Cry, the Beloved Country

Alan Paton

Curriculum Unit

Ruth L. Van Arsdale

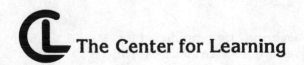
The Center for Learning

Ruth L. VanArsdale, an outstanding secondary English teacher and leader, earned her M.A. at Augustana College, Sioux Falls, South Dakota. She is coauthor of a World Literature curriculum unit and author of a variety of Novel/Drama units including *Wuthering Heights, Gulliver's Travels, Things Fall Apart/No Longer at Ease, Death Comes for the Archbishop,* and *Invisible Man.*

The Publishing Team

Rose Schaffer, M.A., President/Chief Executive Officer
Bernadette Vetter, M.A., Vice President
Diane Podnar, M.S., Production Director

Cover Design

Mary Souders

List of credits found on Acknowledgments
Page beginning on 70.

ISBN 1-56077-213-1

Contents

Introduction

One would think that forty years would date a social-problem novel. Not so with Alan Paton's *Cry, the Beloved Country.* The racial situation portrayed in the book remains much as it was depicted by the author. How close South Africa is to finding a solution and what social upheaval is still ahead are important problems to be faced by the international community. Because our nation has had to deal with the problem of slavery and still must handle tense racial problems, this is a book that should be read and studied by high school students. Supplementary reading and viewing are imperative to update the material and to show readers how prophetic Paton was in his assessment of the South African situation.

The study unit consists of twelve lessons which deal with both the social situation and the literary value of the book. Most of these lessons consider the novel as a whole and can be done only after the reader is able to evaluate the relationship of all the parts. For this reason, the first reading should be rapid. Most people read to find out the ending, and that is legitimate; but just as a complex problem cannot be solved simply and quickly, so a carefully written book cannot be understood adequately by a cursory reading. The lessons direct the students' attention to different facets of the novel and require focused re-reading.

Lessons also require various activities, such as writing, discussion, route mapping, role playing, and supplementary reading. The desired outcome is student interest in a nation whose problems parallel some of our own and today have international implications.

Normally, it is not wise to quote the page on which something can be found, but checking both paperback and hardback copies resulted in finding identical pagination; therefore pages are stated in this unit.

The values stressed in this unit on *Cry, the Beloved Country* are as follows:

- an understanding of the national background that created the setting of the novel
- seeing from both the white and the black viewpoint a racial problem that parallels our nation's
- realizing the destructive power of fear
- understanding the restorative, integrating power of love

Preliminary Notes to the Teacher

Although *Cry, the Beloved Country* was written in 1948, it is an important contemporary novel because South Africa is receiving much more international attention today than it was at the time the novel was written. The races have not followed the example of Stephen Kumalo and James Jarvis: therefore, Msimangu's prediction that the blacks would turn to hatred to attain their civil rights can be verified by reading the daily newspaper, listening to television newscasts, or reading current news magazines.

The unit itself contains no chapter-by-chapter study guide, for the writing is clear and direct, easily understood by the average high school reader. Much of the complexity appears only as one views the work as a whole. For that reason, students should have finished the book before doing Lessons 4–12. Unit Test I should probably be given after Lesson 3, because it deals with points the students should know after a first reading. Unit Test II can well be given at the end of the entire study, for it calls for evaluation that can best be done by those who have contributed to the classroom work throughout the unit and have actively listened to what has developed. Although most discussions are correlated with the handouts in the unit, some students may benefit from taking class notes.

Obviously, the novel could be studied for its social value, but such a study would do injustice to its literary value. Alan Paton carefully treats the views of an elderly black man and his white counterpart, and a young black man and his counterpart. In addition, he uses a three-book structure and several conventional literary devices, making this an interesting book for the high school English class. Finally, because he has created two characters for whom the readers develop a genuine sympathy, he is able, without preaching, to apply to a contemporary situation the scriptural principal, "true love casts out fear."

Small-group and teacher-led classroom discussions are essential for discovering much of the novel's value. Such exploration will reveal many facets not covered in this unit. Students must also read news magazines and newspapers as well as listen to newscasts to understand the latest developments in an explosive situation. Lesson 11 refers to *Kaffir Boy* by Mark Mathabane, a young man who in the summer of 1987 appeared on "Good Morning America" to explain how he came to America and what he hopes to accomplish in helping to liberate South African blacks. That book gives an even more alarming realization of the cruelty caused by fear and the difficulties faced by anyone who seeks for a peaceful solution to the racial problems in South Africa.

Finally, lessons selected should be governed by the needs of a particular class. Activities include writing, discussion, role playing, analysis of grammatical structure, and analysis of literary devices. To use all of them might become tedious for some classes and cause students to feel that detailed study kills the enjoyment of reading.

Lesson 1
Historical and Political Background

Objectives
- To become informed about the background of apartheid in South Africa
- To learn about the political events that shaped the specific backdrop for the novel

Notes to the Teacher

Before understanding what Alan Paton is saying in his novel, beyond merely telling a good story, one must know something of the historical and political background that has made South Africa the troubled nation that it is today.

Using the *Readers' Guide to Periodical Literature*, students can find many articles about the history of South Africa. Some that are particularly good are: "Heading toward a Bloodbath," in *Newsweek* (June 23, 1986); "Moving to Muzzle the Messenger," in *Time* (December 22, 1986); "United No More," in *Time* (May 4, 1987); and "South Africa: Subtle Stakes," in *U.S. News and World Report* (May 11, 1987). Another suggested reading is "A Literary Remembrance," an insightful unfinished essay by Paton which was printed posthumously in *Time* (April 25, 1988).

Handout 1 allows students to focus on several of the important issues that form the background for the novel. It is not exhaustive and therefore should be used chiefly as a springboard for discussion. Obviously, each student will not need to read all the articles available on this very timely subject. In fact, if all will read the introduction that is provided in the paperback edition of the novel and then perhaps the article in *Time* (May 4, 1987), the class will have a common background that will answer most of the questions. Other articles will enhance that knowledge.

Procedure
1. Using **Handout 1**, ask students to answer, in writing, the questions listed. They may work in groups of two or three or individually, according to the discretion of the teacher.

2. After the worksheet is completed, it should be used as the basis for a discussion of South Africa as it was perceived by Alan Paton in 1948, and as analysts see it today. To get a view of geography as students learn of the history, it would be well to have a map of South Africa before the class during this discussion. If such a map is not readily available, the one found in **Handout 3** can be used.

Suggested Responses for **Handout 1**:
1. *Who made the first landing on South African soil? (Jan van Riebeeck of the Dutch East India Company)*
2. *When and where did it take place? (In 1652 at the Cape of Good Hope)*
3. *What natives did they find? (Nomads whom they called Hottentots)*
4. *What happened to these natives? (Most of them died in a smallpox epidemic that came after the landing of a company ship from India)*
5. *After the Dutch were joined by Germans and French Huguenots, whom did they get to do the heavy work? (Slaves that they imported from Madagascar, Mozambique, and the Dutch East Indies)*
6. *How did Africa change these people into what are now known as the Afrikaners? (Although the Dutch, Germans, and French had not intended to settle there, they found fertile valleys and beautiful mountains. They developed homes and eventually their own language, Afrikaans.)*
7. *How did the British become a part of the history of South Africa? (Arriving in 1795, they seized the settlement at Cape Town because they wanted to keep the French from having that port for their India trade.)*
8. *What caused the Afrikaners to make the "Great Trek"? (In the 1830s they moved to an uninhabited wilderness to the northeast along the Vaal River*

because they wanted to escape the discomforts of the British rule, which included a ban on slavery.)

9. What probably began the Afrikaners' sense of being threatened by the black man? (Bantu tribesmen, looking for new lands, came south and clashed with the Afrikaners they found in the area, now known as the Transvaal and the Orange Free State.)

10. What caused the British to invade the area near the Orange River? (In 1867 a diamond was discovered near the Orange River, and the British annexed those lands and sent their miners there to dig for diamonds.)

11. What war did the Afrikaners fight to resist this invasion? (They fought what is now known as the Boer, or farmers', War from 1899–1902.)

12. What kind of warfare did they carry on? (Guerrilla attacks)

13. What word commonly used today came from these fighting tactics? (Commando)

14. What was the outcome of this struggle? (The British overcame the Afrikaners and confined the women and children in concentration camps, where almost a third of them died.)

15. What new country resulted from this war, and what territory did it cover? (The Union of South Africa in 1910, including the Cape of Good Hope, the Orange Free State, the Transvaal, and Natal)

16. What is the Broederbond and what is its importance to this day? (The Brotherhood, a movement that advocated Afrikaner solidarity and separation from both British and blacks)

17. What important person was in 1987 still a member of the Broederbond? (President P. W. Botha)

18. How and why did apartheid become the law of the land? (In 1934 Daniel Malan founded the National Party, and in 1948 he defeated General Smuts in the election. In retaliation against the British, he declared apartheid to be law.)

Assignment
Read Chapters 1-5.

Name _____

Date _____

Gaining Historical Perspective

Directions: If possible, read these articles before answering the questions:
"Heading toward a Bloodbath," NEWSWEEK (June 23, 1986)
"Moving to Muzzle the Messenger," TIME (December 22, 1986)
*"United No More," TIME (May 4, 1987)

The starred article is the most important one for this lesson, but all add much to understanding and will be used sometime in exploring this novel. If these are not available, encyclopedia information will help. The most valuable source may well be the introduction, found in the front of the novel itself.

Answer in writing the following questions as a background for the novel:

1. Who made the first landing on South African soil?

2. When and where did it take place?

3. What natives did they find?

4. What happened to these natives?

5. After the Dutch were joined by Germans and the French Huguenots, whom did they get to do the heavy work? (Be specific.)

6. How did Africa change these white people into what are now known as the Afrikaners?

7. How did the British become a part of the history of South Africa?

8. What caused the Afrikaners to make the "Great Trek"?

9. What probably began the Afrikaners' sense of being threatened by the black man?

10. What caused the British to invade the area near the Orange River?

11. What war did the Afrikaners fight to resist this invasion?

12. What kind of warfare did they carry on?

13. What word commonly used today comes from these fighting tactics?

14. What was the outcome of this struggle?

15. What new country resulted from this war, and what territory did it cover?

16. What is the Broederbond, and what is its importance to this day?

17. What important person was still in 1987 a member of the Broederbond?

18. How and why did apartheid become the law of the land?

Lesson 2
Setting

Objectives

- To note details that form the physical setting
- To detect the mood created by this setting

Notes to the Teacher

Alan Paton very carefully creates a landscape that is lush and green. However, as the readers look through the eyes of the narrator toward the valley below, they see that the soil is red and eroded; no longer can it produce the crops needed to support the people. Furthermore, no rain has come to water the valley. The mood is immediately one of discouragement and privation.

Handout 2 requires a careful reading of chapters 1-5, with a study of chapters 1 and 4. The work can be done individually, followed by a class discussion, or it can be done as a class, students filling in their handouts as the discovery session proceeds. Teacher discretion will determine the specific method that best fits the class situation.

Procedure

1. Distribute **Handout 2.**

2. Direct students to a silent reading of Chapter 1 or read it aloud as students follow in their books. It is better to read the chapter in its entirety before searching for the answers to specific questions. Fill in answers by whatever method you find best for the class.

3. Distribute **Handout 3,** directing students to draw their free-hand map and then mark in color the route that Kumalo takes in going from Ixopo to Johannesburg. Point out Pretoria to them as well, for it will have importance later in the book. Warn them that of the places named in Chapter 4, they will probably find only three. If they look at the first paragraph of

Chapter 23, they will find out approximately where the gold mining district is to be found. Obviously, with the valleys mentioned, the train did not take a straight, "as the crow flies" route, but the main point of this exercise is to give some feeling of where the story takes place.

Suggested responses for **Handout 2**

1. *Read the first two paragraphs. List three adjectives you could use to describe the Umzimkulu Valley. (Answers will vary, but some possibilities are rich, lovely, grassy, green, lush, fertile.)*

2. *Now read the third paragraph. What has happened to the lower hills and the second valley? (They have been exploited by too much grazing and field burning. As a result, they are eroded and unproductive.)*

3. *Read the fourth paragraph. What has happened to the families that once lived on the land? (They are broken, for the women and children are left to eke out an existence, while the men and boys have gone to the cities to work.)*

4. *Read the first five paragraphs of Chapter 4. Compare the soil of the great valley of the Umkomaas with the Umzimkulu Valley of Chapter 1. (The "soil is sick almost beyond healing." If anything, the condition is worse here.)*

5. *The city of Pietermaritzburg is Alan Paton's birthplace. Until he died in 1988, he lived in the same province, Natal, but in the city of Hillcrest. What adjective does he use to describe his birthplace? (Lovely)*

6. *Notice also that this first reference to Afrikaans is that it is "a language he [Stephen Kumalo] had never yet heard spoken." What does that say about the place from which he comes? (It is isolated, largely left alone by white people.)*

7. What industry is carried on in the part of the land where Stephen first hears Afrikaans spoken? (Gold mining)

8. Read on through the second page of Chapter 4. What is Kumalo's first impression of this industry? (He is over-awed by the great wheel that goes so fast that the "spokes play tricks with the sight.")

9. Finish Chapter 4. What is Kumalo's initial impression of Johannesburg? (It is a frightening place with high buildings. He sees also a giant billboard with a bottle that tips to fill a glass and then sits upright again. When he gets off the train, he joins the throng of people coming and going in an underground tunnel. After he climbs the stairs and reaches the street, he does not dare to cross even though the light is green because a bus swings into his path. Immediately he is taken in by a young man who takes his money on the pretense of buying him a ticket. A kind man takes him to Sophiatown, where he meets Mr. Msimangu and admits that he is "much confused.")

10. What contrasts are there between the land in Chapter 1 and the city in Chapter 4? (Answers will vary.)

11. What impressions do these chapters give you of South Africa? (Answers will vary.)

12. Find specific examples that show what Stephen Kumalo's experiences and reactions reveal about the racial situation and white supremacy in South Africa. (Answers will vary, but basically the Zulu has lived apart from the white man on depleted land. No one has cared to teach him land conservation methods. He is frightened and intimidated by the city. When he moves from place to place, he encounters a language barrier; therefore he is a foreigner except in his own small village. When Kumalo takes the train, he must get in the car for non-Europeans because white and black are segregated.)

Suggested responses for **Handout 3**

After drawing the free-hand map, students should have located the three places mentioned: Ixopo (Chapter 4), Pietermaritzburg, and Johannesburg. Chapter 4 mentions other towns that probably cannot be found on maps they locate in the library. Next they need to refer to the first paragraph of Chapter 23, where they will learn that gold was found in Odendaalsrust in Orange Free State. The train, on its way to Johannesburg, probably went not too far from that place, which can be located on the map and marked with an X. Pretoria should also be noted because it is there that Absalom is imprisoned (Chapter 32). Though not pinpointing the trip accurately, the exercise should give the students some geographical perspective. If one takes into consideration the mountainous terrain, the trip probably covered about 300 miles.

Assignment
Finish Book I (Chapters 6-17)

A Land of Contrast

Directions: Write answers to the following questions:

1. Read the first two paragraphs of the story. List *three* adjectives that you could use to describe the Umzimkulu Valley.

   a.

   b.

   c.

2. Now read the third paragraph. What has happened to the lower hills and the second valley?

3. Read the fourth paragraph. What has happened to the families who once lived there?

4. Read the first five paragraphs of Chapter 4. Compare the soil of the great valley of the Umkomaas to the Umzimkulu Valley of Chapter 1.

5. The city of Pietermaritzburg is Alan Paton's birthplace. Until he died in 1988, he lived in the same province, Natal, but in the city of Hillcrest. What adjective does he use to describe his birthplace?

6. Notice that his first reference to Afrikaans is that it is "a language he [Stephen Kumalo] had never yet heard spoken. What does that say about the place from which Stephen comes?

7. What industry is carried on in that part of the land where Stephen first hears Afrikaans spoken?

8. Read on through the second page of Chapter 4. What is Kumalo's first impression of this industry?

9. Finish Chapter 4. What is Kumalo's initial impression of Johannesburg?

10. What contrasts are there between the land in Chapter 1 and the city in Chapter 4?

11. What impressions do these chapters give you of South Africa?

12. Find specific examples that show what Stephen Kumalo's experiences and reactions reveal about the racial situation and white supremacy in South Africa. List at least five.

   a.

   b.

   c.

   d.

   e.

Name _____

Date _____

Mapping a Journey

Directions: After studying maps in a large atlas (*World Book* Encyclopedia also has an excellent one under the heading "Union of South Africa"), draw a free-hand map of South Africa. You will find the account of Kumalo's train trip in Chapter 4. Not all the places mentioned can be found on your map, but three important points are Ixopo, Pietermaritzburg, and Johannesburg. Notice also that he goes through the gold-mining province called Orange Free State. Look in Chapter 23 for the city near which his train probably traveled. Draw an *X* to locate that city. Now draw a colored line that would show approximately what Kumalo's route was. Of course his trip was more circuitous than can be shown by straight lines on a map, for some of the time he traveled in mountainous country. Approximately how many miles did he travel in somewhat over twenty-four hours?

Lesson 3

Style

Objectives

- To analyze specific features of Alan Paton's style of writing
- To observe how style and content are related

Notes to the Teacher

High school students are not prepared to do an in-depth analysis of style, for it is a very elusive aspect of fiction. However, Paton's style suits his material so well that one cannot ignore the need for appreciating how each complements the other. Style will not be approached in general but will be seen through specific ways that Paton handles narration, description, and dialogue; through the rhythms of his language and examples of his phraseology.

Procedure

1. Distribute **Handout 4.** Because some students may have difficulty with this lesson, the instructor may wish to handle it as a teacher-directed discussion. The students should, however, be led to discover the particulars rather than to be told them in lecture.

2. Distribute **Handout 5.** This activity should be done individually or in small groups, followed by discussion before the final paragraph writing is done.

Suggested responses for **Handout 4**

1. *What is style as applied to a literary work? (Any good handbook may be used for arriving at a definition. Basically it is the arrangement of words in such a way that they suit a particular author's intent and personality.)*

2. *Turn to Chapter 2. How does Paton punctuate dialogue? (At the end of the first paragraph, he simply puts a comma and then the speaker's words. When more than one person speaks, a dash precedes each response; no quotation marks occur.)*

3. *What does that punctuation do for the story? (Answers will vary, but one explanation is that it keeps the conversation moving. Since the people address each other as "umfundisi" and "small one," there is no problem with knowing who is speaking. Also the economy of punctuation and wording fits the poverty of the situation.)*

4. *Notice the relative formality of the child's speech and actions. What does it reveal about the Zulu people living in Ndotsheni? (They are not the savages many have stereotyped them to be. There is also a deep respect for elders, especially leaders in the community.)*

5. *What does Paton's use of actual place names and some Afrikaan and Zulu words do for the story? (These give an authenticity to a fictional story, making one believe the experience is actual.)*

6. *Turn back to Chapter 1 to read paragraphs 1 and 2. Now turn to Chapter 18, the beginning of Book II, paragraphs 1 and 2. What is obviously true of these two passages? (They are identical except Chapter 1 has two extra sentences, beginning with "Stand unshod.")*

7. *Read on in Chapter 18 to see who is viewing the scene this time. What does the repetition with a new observer do for the novel? (It connects the two books and parallels the experience of the black person who appears to be seeing it in Chapter 1 with that of the white man who later views it, apparently James Jarvis.)*

8. *Critics have at times noted the poetic qualities of the passages referred to above.*

a. *List some of the images that could be considered poetic. ("grass-covered and rolling, no mist, grass and bracken, forlorn crying of the titihoya, on its journey, to the sea, beyond and behind" [repeated])*

b. *List three of the phrases that are made up of parallel words joined by and. ("Rich and matted, the rain and the mist, grass-covered and rolling")*
   What poetic quality do you detect? (Rhythm)

c. *What might the author be saying by using such a poetic setting in contrast with the novel's events? (The land is beautiful and has potential for nourishing productive life, but man's greed and destructive nature have corrupted the Edenic environment.)*

d. *What mood do these passages create? (A mood of awe tinged by sadness)*

e. *What kind of story might one anticipate from these descriptions? (A sad story that reveals man's destructiveness, but a kind of beauty pervading in spite of the general decay.)*

9. *Another sad poem is found in Chapter 9 (p. 54), beginning with "—Have you a room to let?" List at least three poetic features of that short section. (Repetition of the word let, rhythm of lines, parallel patterns joined by taken away and corrupted by, and the summarizing fragment, "But my husband gets only thirty-four shillings a week—")*

10. *A prose-poem is found toward the end of that chapter (p. 57). It is composed of three paragraphs, each beginning with "Shanty Town is up overnight." What poetic characteristic much like that of Walt Whitman is found in this passage? (Cataloging of details, as well as the short phrase and repetition. Especially noticeable are "Squatters they call us. We are the squatters" and "Quietly my child, your mother is by you. Quietly my child, do not cough any more, your mother is by you.")*

11. *Even in those passages that are strictly prose, Paton writes with great conciseness. One example is found in Chapter 5 (p. 22, paragraph 2). It begins, "So they all talked of the sickness of the land." List at least three details about the African situation that you learn from this short summary paragraph. (Tribes and homes are broken, young people are lawless, whites are afraid of blacks in Johannesburg.)*

12. *Find two other examples of Paton's concise style. Why did you choose them as your examples? (Answers will vary.)*

13. *In a paper of 300-500 words, relate how Paton's style fits the African setting and situation. Briefly explain what you have observed about his handling of dialogue, his use of Zulu and Afrikaan words and names, his repetition of the opening scene, his poetic passages, and his conciseness of exposition. Then show how this style fits his subject.*

Suggested responses for Handout 5

1. *One other feature of Paton's style is his directness, as evidenced by an uncomplicated sentence structure that nevertheless uses some complexity and a great deal of variety. Consider first the eleven sentences in paragraphs 1 and 2 of the novel. Label each as to type: simple, compound, complex, or compound-complex. Label also participial phrases, appositives, and parallel series.*

   a. *Complex*
   b. *Compound*
   c. *Compound-complex*
   d. *Compound with added appositive*
   e. *Compound (last two clauses have an implied is)*
   f. *Compound*
   g. *Compound with added participial phrase (feeling . . . kloof)*
   h. *Compound with participial phrase (laying bare the soil)*
   i. *Compound with participial phrase (being . . . Creator)*

j. Compound with parallel series, each beginning with a verb

k. Compound

2. Are there any simple sentences? (No) Why would you probably not have said that immediately after a quick reading and before analyzing the structure? (The feeling is that the sentences are short; smooth, and uncomplicated.) How does his style suit his material? (He is describing a complex situation that appears simple on the surface. At first one thinks this is a Garden of Eden, but quickly the reader finds that something has gone wrong. One sees an intricate weaving of reasons.)

3. After reading the last paragraph on p. 99 (Chapter 14), beginning with "And again the tears," analyze the types of sentence units. In addition to labeling as to type, label the series as verb, infinitive, word list, or short clause. Tell also whether each is a question or a statement.

   a. Fragment

   b. Question (complex)

   c. Question (complex)

   d. Question (complex, using also a series of verb phrases)

   e. Question (complex, using a series of infinitive phrases, a series of why's, and ending with an adverb clause)

   f. Compound sentence, using a series of short clauses, a series of words, and a series that lists people)

4. What is the effect of the passage just analyzed? (It creates a feeling that the procedure of law and even of human desire to know the motivation of another is endless and rather futile.)

5. After reading the paragraph just before the break on p. 123 (Chapter 17), beginning "so Kumalo left him," analyze the sentences as before, noting both type and structure.

   a. Compound with added adjective and infinitive phrase (ready, to come in)

   b. Compound with prepositional and participial phrases (like a man, used to heavy matters)

   c. Compound-complex with adjective, elliptical clause, and prepositional phrase (much greater, than the case, of a boy)

6. Usually one would be told not to begin a paragraph with so and not to use and repeatedly as the connective for the compound sentences. Why do these features work so well for Paton here? (They create a feeling of simplicity at the same time that the constructions themselves give a great number of details in a very short space.)

7. In a paragraph describe the seeming simplicity but actual complexity of Paton's style. Then in a second paragraph tell why this style is well suited to his material. (Because the sentences appear short, one would expect many of them to be simple, but analysis shows they are not. Examples should be cited to verify this statement. The style suits the content, for the stereotypical American picture of Africa is that the people live a simple, uncomplicated life. Yet here are complexities greater than most of us face. Apartheid alone defies world solution.)

Assignment

Read Books II and III (Chapters 18-36).

Name _____

Date _____

Paton's Style

Directions: Answer the following questions:

1. What is style as applied to a literary work?

2. Turn to Chapter 2. How does Paton punctuate dialogue?

3. What does that punctuation do for the story?

4. Notice the relative formality of the child's speech and actions. What does it reveal about the Zulu people living in Ndotsheni?

5. What does Paton's use of actual place names and some Afrikaan and Zulu words do for the story?

6. Go back to Chapter 1 to read paragraphs 1 and 2. Now turn to Chapter 18, the beginning of Book II, to read paragraphs 1 and 2. What is obviously true of these two passages?

7. Read on in Chapter 18 to see who is viewing the scene this time. What does this repetition with a new observer do for the novel?

8. Critics have at times noted the poetic qualities of the passages referred to above.

   a. List at least five images that could be considered poetic.

   b. List three of the phrases that are made up of parallel words joined by *and*. What poetic characteristic do you detect?

   c. What might the author be saying by using such a poetic setting in contrast with the novel's events?

   d. What mood do these passages create?

   e. What kind of story might one anticipate from these descriptions?

9. A very sad poem is found in Chapter 9 (p. 54), beginning with "—Have you a room to let?" List at least three poetic features of that short section

10. A prose-poem is found toward the end of that chapter (p. 57). It is made up of three paragraphs, each beginning with "Shanty Town is up overnight." What poetic characteristic much like that of Walt Whitman is found in this passage?

11. Even in those passages that are strictly prose, Paton writes with great conciseness what he wishes to say. One example is found in Chapter 5 (p. 22, paragraph 2). It begins, "So they all talked of the sickness of the land." List at least three details about the African situation that you learn from this short summary paragraph.

12. Find two other examples of Paton's concise style. Why did you pick them as your examples?

13. In a paper of 300-500 words, briefly explain what you have observed about Paton's handling of dialogue, his use of Zulu and Afrikaan words and names, his repetition of the opening scene, his poetic passages, and his conciseness of exposition. Then show how his style fits his subject.

Name _____

Date _____

Simply Complex

Directions: Answer the questions:

1. One other feature of Paton's style is his directness, as evidenced by an uncomplicated sentence structure that nevertheless uses some complexity and a great deal of variety. Consider first the eleven sentences in paragraphs 1 and 2 of the novel. Label each as to type: simple, compound, complex, or compound-complex. Also label participial phrases, appositives, and parallel series.

   a.

   b.

   c.

   d.

   e.

   f.

   g.

   h.

   i.

   j.

   k.

2. Are there any simple sentences? (yes, no) Why would you probably not have said that immediately after a quick reading and before analyzing the structure?

3. After reading the last paragraph on p. 99 (Chapter 14), beginning with "And again the tears," analyze the types of sentence units. In addition to labeling as to type, label the series as *verb, infinitive, word list, or short clause.* Tell also whether each is a question or a statement.

   a.

   b.

   c.

   d.

   e.

   f.

4. What is the effect of the passage just analyzed? What feeling does it create?

5. After reading the paragraph just before the break on p. 123 (chapter 17), beginning "So Kumalo left him," analyze the sentences as before, noting both type and structure.

   a.

   b.

   c.

6. Usually one would be told not to begin a paragraph with *so* and not to use *and* repeatedly as the connective for the compound sentences. Why do these features work so well for Paton here?

7. In a paragraph, describe the seeming simplicity but actual complexity of Paton's style. In a second paragraph tell why this style is well suited to his material.

Lesson 4

Structure

Objectives

- To examine the three-book structure of the novel
- To determine what is accomplished by this plan of development

Notes to the Teacher

It is not certain what Paton intended with the three-book structure of his novel; nevertheless, an examination of that plan gives some interesting possibilities and can be a worthwhile small-group discovery process. It is likely best that the groups be composed of three or at the most four persons to insure that all actively participate. Eventually the teacher will enter the process, but it is probably better that students be given half the class time to work without teacher input.

Procedure

1. Divide the class into groups, perhaps having in each group at least one creative thinker and one student who needs the leadership of the others to comprehend the activity. The other one or two can be average students.

2. Distribute **Handout 6,** instructing students that they are to answer the questions in writing only after they have discussed possibilities. There are no correct answers, only those that are formed after thoughtful consideration.

3. After dividing the class into two groups, distribute **Handout 7.** One group is to construct a case against Matthew Kumalo and Johannes Pafuri for inciting a riot and in that riot beating up a white law officer, injuring him so gravely that he may never be able to work again. The other is to construct the defense they would present.

Suggested Responses for Handout 6

Listed below are the basic conflicts found in literature:

a. *the struggle against the forces of nature*
b. *the struggle against another person*
c. *the struggle against society as a force*
d. *the struggle of two elements for mastery within oneself*
e. *the struggle against fate or destiny*

1. *Which of these conflicts can be found in Book I? Within whom is each found? (Answers will vary.)*
2. *Which of these conflicts are found in Book II? Within whom? (Answers will vary.)*
3. *Why can one not say that the basic conflict is white vs. black? (Jarvis and Kumalo are never really against one another; neither are Arthur and Absalom: Arthur worked for the good of the black people, and Absalom had never intended to kill Arthur.)*
4. *What then is the dominant conflict? How are both black and white losers in the struggle? Is there any victory? (The dominant conflict is man vs. society as a force. Jarvis and Kumalo lose their sons to the evils of that societal structure; Arthur and Absalom lose their lives. A partial solution comes through men like the young man at the reformatory, who tries to help; Carmichael, who takes the case "for God"; and the black priest Msimangu, who renounces material things for a life of meditation and prayer. Victory comes in one small village, Ndotsheni, where black and white unite to better living conditions.)*

5. *What event in Book II becomes the climax, if you consider both the point of highest emotional interest and the point at which one force wins out and the rising action reverses and becomes the falling action? (The judgment in Chapter 28, (page 201), is most likely the climax; for it is the high point of emotion. Though the verdict is no surprise to the readers, they have become so involved with Kumalo that they wish the death penalty could have been avoided, particularly since Absalom's killing of Arthur was not premeditated and the other two young men are acquitted. Society has been established as the dominant force, the winner over Kumalo and the people of his race. The rising action is reversed and becomes the falling action.)*

6. *Although Book III is a part of the falling action, it also becomes the beginning of a solution to society's ills. What is the force that has overcome the fear that each race has had for the other? (Love)*

7. *This is a problem novel, somewhat akin to the problem play, in that the protagonist is confronted by social problems and issues. If it were considered as a three-act problem play with each book being one act, what is contributed by each act? Is any part of the problem solved? If so, how? (Answers will vary.)*

Suggested responses for **Handout 7**
(These will, of course, vary. It would be interesting after the cases are built to hold a trial. There will need to be a judge, the attorneys, the defendants, and witnesses on both sides. Perhaps the bailiff, clerk of court, and court reporter could be the same person. the rest of the class will be jury. The whole class should help in planning the case so that everyone is vitally involved.)

Name _____

Date _____

Man and Society in Conflict

Directions. Listed below are the basic conflicts found in literature:

a. the struggle against the forces of nature

b. the struggle against another person

c. the struggle against society as a force

d. the struggle of two elements for mastery within oneself

e. the struggle against fate or destiny

On a separate sheet of paper answer the questions:

1. Which of these conflicts can be found in Book I? Within whom is each found? Which conflict appears to be the most important?

2. Which of these conflicts can be found in Book II? Within whom is each found?

3. Why can one not say that the basic conflict is white vs. black?

4. What then is the dominant conflict? How are both black and white losers in the struggle? Is there any victory?

5. What event in Book II becomes the climax, if you consider both the point of highest emotional interest and the point at which one force wins out and the rising action reverses itself and becomes the falling action?

6. Although Book III is part of the falling action, it also becomes the beginning of a solution to society's ills. What is the force that has overcome the fear that each race has had for the other?

7. This is a problem novel, somewhat akin to the problem play, in that the protagonist is confronted by social problems and issues. If it were considered as a three-act problem play with each book being one act, what is contributed by each act? Is any part of the problem solved? If so, how?

Name _____

Date _____

The State vs. Kumalo and Pafuri

Directions: After the class has been divided into two groups, each group will build one of the following cases. You may have to consult at first to determine what the actual injuries to the officer were.

1. Construct a case against Matthew Kumalo and Johannes Pafuri for inciting a riot and in that riot beating up a white law officer, injuring him so gravely that he may never be able to work again.

2. Construct the defense Matthew Kumalo and Johannes Pafuri's lawyer will present.

Lesson 5
Point of View

Objectives

- To discover from what point of view the story is told
- To determine the advantages of using that point of view

Notes to the Teacher

In Thrall and Hibbard, *A Handbook to Literature* (New York: The Odyssey Press, 1961—revised and enlarged edition), *point of view* is defined as follows:

> A term used in the analysis and criticism of FICTION to describe the way in which the reader is presented with the materials of the story, or, viewed from another angle, the vantage point from which the author presents the action of the story. The author may tell the story in the third person and yet present it as it is seen and understood by a single character—major, minor, or merely witness—restricting information to what that character sees, hears, feels, and thinks. (p. 371)

Students who are accustomed to third-person omniscient point of view need to be aware of the above addition, which is usually called the third-person limited. Paton sometimes causes us to see things as Kumalo does, then as Jarvis does, and suddenly as an outside observer does. He makes these changes so smoothly that it is beneficial to observe at what points he shifts. Some students may readily recognize the fact that the device is something like the television camera that focuses sometimes on one person, then on another, and finally on the whole room.

Procedure

1. Review the basics of point of view, defining the following:
   a. First-person narrator (One person tells the story, limiting the reader's understanding to what he/she perceives.)
   b. Naive or disingenuous narrator (He/She does not comprehend the implications of what is happening.)
   c. Third-person omniscient (The all-knowing author has no restrictions of time, place, or character and therefore moves freely and comments at will.)
   d. Third-person limited (The author uses the viewpoint of more than one person but limits himself/herself at any one time to what only one person sees or feels.)

2. As a class, deal with the overall point of view from which Paton tells his story (third-person limited)

3. Divide the class into three groups, assigning one book of the novel to each group.

4. Distribute **Handout 8**, instructing each group to deal with the one book assigned to it.

Suggested responses to Handout 8

Book I
   A. *Beginning with Chapter 2, whose viewpoint predominates? (Kumalo's)*
   B. *What is this person's vocation? (Minister)*
   C. *State at least two advantages of using that person's point of view. (He is relatively free to move about the country, for he is not a day laborer. He is from the country and therefore sees the city for the first time. Because he is older, he is not dazzled by the city. As a minister, he is interested in moral issues.*
   D. *List African social and economic conditions that become clear to the reader through Kumalo's eyes. (Answers will vary.)*

Book II
   A. *From whose viewpoint do we now see the setting identical to that found in Chapter 1? (James Jarvis, Esquire)*
   B. *How does he see the agricultural situation? (He sees the dry land in need of rain, the green grass at the tops, and finally the black man's land that Jarvis wishes had been farmed better.)*

C. What is the advantage of seeing the African landscape and the murder of Arthur Jarvis from his point of view? (He sees things from an educated, white Englishman's perspective. Also, since he is Arthur's father, he has access to his son's letters and other papers relating to work done for the good of the black people. He also displays a white father's grief and his growing realization that the average white man is far removed from the black man's plight.)

D. Beginning with Chapter 22, the narrator becomes the impartial observer. What things do you learn about Africa in Chapters 22 and 23? (Answers will vary, but some possibilities are that it is a land of fear; the white man makes the law; the black man has little chance in the courts; gold and greed for riches take precedence over concern about a murdered white man; the rich man is respected regardless of how he uses others as work animals. Finally, the narrator sounds disgusted with the whole situation when he says that one Johannesburg is enough in the world.)

E. From whose viewpoint is most of Chapter 24 told? (James Jarvis') Why is it better to use his viewpoint rather than Kumalo's when telling of their first face-to-face meeting? (We can notice the slow revelation of their having something in common, since he does not recognize Kumalo immediately; we can see how it is possible for Arthur to have developed such a concern for black people when we see the compassion of his father.)

F. From Chapter 26 to the end of Book II, whose viewpoint is used? (The impartial observer) Why is this point of view effective? (The emotional impact of Kumalo's meeting with Jarvis is important, for they are the people we identify with. A reporter's style is better for the trial, for this is the iron hand of the law, a cold society judging without heart. Also a new element is added, John Kumalo's inciting the people. This scene could not be reported as well by either Kumalo or Jarvis.

The scene between father and son could very easily become maudlin if not told with detachment. It is more starkly real and heart breaking when understated in this way. The same is true of Stephen Kumalo's facing his brother and his realizing that Gertrude will not change.)

Book III
A. Through whose eyes are we viewing this situation? (Kumalo's)
B. What philosophy of life comes to us in Chapter 30? Find at least two quotations that state this philosophy. ("Kindness and love can pay for pain and suffering." and "there is no life without suffering.")
C. Chapter 31 begins with the fact that Kumalo prays regularly but also comes to an important realization. What is that realization? (Praying must be supplemented by action. People must unite across racial lines.)
D. From what viewpoint are Chapters 32 and 33 told? (Impartial observer) Why is this viewpoint effective? (There is much exposition requiring an outside observer: Absalom must die, the land is surveyed, Jarvis and Kumalo meet again, the valley situation is bettered by the milk, Kumalo continues to teach Jarvis' grandson, and the young man explains about the dam. No one person could have handled all this, for much territory and many types of events are covered. If Kumalo's viewpoint had been used, the emotion of Absalom's death sentence would probably have dominated everything else, and that is not the purpose of this section. The situation is larger than any one man's grief.)
E. The final three chapters narrow our vision back to one man, Stephen Kumalo. What is the advantage of ending the book in this manner? (We started with his viewpoint; his experiences in Johannesburg have broadened his perspective; now we have come full circle. It gives the narrator

the opportunity to sum up the situation through an individual's thoughts; for example, he recalls Msimangu's prediction of today's situation: "I have one great fear in my heart, that one day when they turn to loving they will find that we are turned to hating.")

Name _____

Date _____

Point of View

Directions: Join the group to which you have been assigned to find answers to the questions about the book section assigned to you. In class discussion afterward, you will be given answers to questions on the other two sections of the book. Please use your own paper.

Book I

A. Beginning with Chapter 2, whose viewpoint predominates?

B. What is this person's vocation?

C. State at least two advantages of using that person's point of view.

D. List African social and economic conditions that become clear to the reader through his eyes.

Book II

A. From whose viewpoint do we now see the setting identical to that found in Chapter 1?

B. How does he see the agricultural situation?

C. What is the advantage of seeing the African landscape and the murder of Arthur Jarvis from his point of view?

D. Beginning with Chapter 22, the narrator becomes the impartial observer. What things do you learn about Africa in Chapters 22 and 23?

E. From whose viewpoint is most of Chapter 24 told? Why is it better to use his viewpoint rather than Kumalo's when telling of their first meeting?

F. From Chapter 26 to the end of Book II, whose viewpoint is used? Why is this point of view effective?

Book III

A. Through whose eyes are we viewing the situation at the beginning of this section?

B. What philosophy of life comes to us in Chapter 30? Find at least two quotations that state this philosophy.

C. Chapter 31 begins with the fact that Kumalo prays regularly but also comes to an important realization. What is that realization?

D. From what viewpoint are Chapter 32 and 33 written? Why is this viewpoint effective?

E. The final three chapters narrow our vision again to that of one man, Stephen Kumalo. What is the advantage of ending the book in this manner?

Lesson 6
Theme

Objective

- To ascertain how Alan Paton develops his stated theme

Notes to the Teacher

In the introduction to the novel, Alan Paton implies his theme. To reduce his statement to terms manageable by high-school students, one must recognize that it deals basically with man's inhumanity to man. However, when man has done all he can to destroy both the land and his fellow human beings, there comes in this story a unification of white and black and a shower of rain to revitalize the earth. The class should realize these points through an inductive process, not through a lecture approach.

Procedure

1. Distribute **Handout 9.** To answer question 1, guide students in reading Alan Paton's implied theme; then let the class "brainstorm" to come up with the common universal theme that is described by Paton and others. (Suggested response is man's inhumanity to man.) If they respond immediately with *prejudice*, help them explore the causes of prejudice. After the bare labeling of the theme, the class may proceed as a whole or in groups of three or four to complete **Handout 9.**

2. Distribute **Handout 10.** Again establish small groups or use the same grouping as for **Handout 9.** Using the pages listed and others, ask each group to develop a collage on one of the suggested themes.

   Suggested Responses for **Handout 9**
   1. *Consider what the author and others have stated in the introduction about the theme; then reduce their ideas to a statement that tells what they are saying about mankind. Your final generalization should be one phrase or one sentence. (Man's inhumanity to man)*

2. *Give examples from the book of the kind of treatment suggested by this theme. (Answers will vary.)*
3. *What does the novel repeatedly show to be the cause of such treatment? (Fear)*
4. *List actions taken by Stephen Kumalo that show him to be different from the people who fit this theme. (Again answers will vary. He is afraid, as the others are, but his faith has taught him that retaliation is not the path to victory.)*
5. *What events cause James Jarvis to see the plight of the black people in Ndotsheni? (Answers will vary, but two that certainly should be considered are his reading of Arthur's manuscripts and his grandson's rides to Kumalo's home, where he learns that the children need milk. Kumalo's humble attitude when he sees James Jarvis at the home of Barbara Smith (Chapter 25) is also undoubtedly an important event.)*
6. *What events at the end of the novel imply a solution to the truth stated in the theme? (Black and white are working together at least in one small part of the country to better the lot of the poor.)*
7. *What is the one quality that can eliminate the cause spoken of in question 3 above? (Love)*
8. *What, if anything, has changed in the social structure between black and white in Ndotsheni? (Nothing has really changed. Kumalo calls Jarvis' grandson "little master," even though he is just a boy. Jarvis is the benevolent white father giving to the poor black man; however, the motivation of love growing from understanding and a commonality of experience may be the seed needed for growth and eventual change.)*
9. *Of what significance is it that Jarvis' grandson wants to learn the Zulu*

language? Think beyond this as merely a device to get Jarvis to help Kumalo. (The father's death may not be in vain, for the son may follow in his footsteps; and the grandfather's heart, softened by his son's death, may give the needed support for continued progress. Also there is the implication that reform in Johannesburg may be a generation or more away. Maybe the boy's generation will act.)

10. Note the guarded optimism of the final paragaraph. Before a real dawn of understanding can come to Africa, what are the specific changes that will liberate white and black from "the fear of bondage and the bondage of fear"? What bondages does each race fear today, and what fears hold each in bondage? (Answers will vary.)

Suggested Responses for **Handout** 10
1. Using the pages listed below and others, if applicable, list the things about which people in South Africa were afraid.
2. Make a collage that is a visual representation of those fears, using both pictures and words,
-or-
3. Make a collage, one half showing fear and the other half showing its antidote. Use the second listing of pages to develop this collage. Pages suggested for the fear collage are the following:

p.14 (the unknown)
p.29 (detection)
p.46 (police, law)
p.49 (trouble)
pp.73,4 (broken land)
p.75 (native crime)
p.76 (blacks in general)
p.79 (possessions, white supremacy)
p.87 (A's whereabouts and actions)
p.88 (broken tribe)
p.89 (everything-fear and pain)
p.96 (John's fear for son)
p.98 (physical safety)
p.106 (anxiety turned to deep fear)
p.111 (fear of parental figure)
pp.162, 3, & 7 (motivation to kill)
p.166 (facing one's victim)
p.189 (ways of the outside world)
p.192 (headlines about violence)
p.198 (secret knowledge)
p.207 (hanging)
p.211 (betrayal)
p.216 (night, death)
p.224 (facing friends)
p.237 (molestation charge)
p.246 (white man's anger)
p.249 (danger to loved one)
p.259 (superior's decision)
p.265 (native chief)
p.275 (taking action for change)
p.277 ("The fear of bondage and the bondage of fear")

Pages to examine for antidote side of second collage:
p.158 (law as stability for whites)
p.180 (understanding and freedom from anger)
p.223 (prayer)
p.225 (God's saving mercy)
p.276 (love)
p.277 (dawning yet unknown and uncertain)

Name _____

Date _____

Theme

Directions: Write answers to the questions, using your own paper.

1. Consider what the author has stated at the end of the first full paragraph on page xviii of his introduction; then reduce that lengthy passage to what it is saying about mankind. Your final generalization should be one phrase or one sentence.
2. Give examples from the book of the kind of treatment suggested by this theme.
3. What does the novel repeatedly show to be the cause of such treatment?
4. List actions taken by Stephen Kumalo that show him to be different from the people who fit this theme.
5. What events cause James Jarvis to see the plight of the black people in Ndotsheni?
6. What events at the end of the novel imply a solution to the truth stated in the theme?
7. What is the one quality that can eliminate the cause spoken of in question 3 above?
8. What, if anything, has changed in the social structure between black and white in Ndotsheni?
9. Of what significance is it that Jarvis' grandson wants to learn the Zulu language? Think beyond this as merely a device to get Jarvis to help Kumalo.
10. Note the guarded optimism of the final paragraph. Before a real dawn of understanding can come to Africa, what are the specific changes that will liberate white and black from "the fear of bondage and the bondage of fear"? What bondages does each race fear today, and what fears hold each in bondage?

Name _____

Date _____

A Picture of Fear

Directions: Carry out the following activities:

1. Using the pages listed below and others, state in a word or phrase the things about which people in South Africa were afraid.

p.14	p.207
p.29	p.211
p.46	p.216
p.49	p.224
pp.73,4	p.237
p.75	p.246
p.76	p.249
p.79	p.259
p.87	p.265
p.88	p.275
p.89	p.277
p.96	
p.98	
p.106	Pages to examine for an antidote to fear:
p.111	
pp.162, 3, & 7	p.158
p.166	p.180
p.189	p.223
p.192	p.225
p.198	p.276
	p.277

2. Make a collage that is a visual representation of those fears, using both pictures and words.

or

3. Make a collage, one half showing *fear* and the other half showing its antidote. Use both listings of pages to develop this collage.

Lesson 7

Characterization

Objectives

- To ascertain Paton's method for characterization
- To observe how this method suits the theme of the novel

Notes to the Teacher

Kumalo can perhaps be termed the protagonist, but Jarvis can certainly not be the antagonist, nor can any other particular person be found in that role. It is probably more accurate to say that the author has created parallel lives: two men, one black and one white, who have lost a son. The loss brings them together to create a bond that surpasses the common experience of grief. In their unity they find comfort for themselves and a new purpose for living by finding an interracial unity, at least in one country village. There are other parallels as well, but the only other one really dealt with in this lesson will be that between Arthur Jarvis and Absalom Kumalo.

Procedure

1. Divide the class into four groups, each finding important personality traits and philosophical ideas of one of the following characters:
   a. Stephen Kumalo (major character)
   b. Absalom Kumalo (minor character)
   c. James Jarvis (major character)
   d. Arthur Jarvis (minor character)

2. Ask the groups to report what they have found, with the rest of the class taking notes on each report.

3. Distribute **Handout** 11. Instruct students to answer each question individually. Compare findings in a large-group discussion.

4. After completing the activities for **Handout** 11, discuss the fact that two minor characters, John Kumalo and his sister Gertrude, have a profound effect on Stephen Kumalo. Since he is their brother and he sees the error of their ways, he wishes to help them. After a brief discussion of how their weaknesses contrast with Stephen's strength, distribute **Handout** 12 for script writing and duet role playing.

Suggested responses for **Handout** 11

1. *In what way are James Jarvis and Stephen Kumalo different? (Jarvis is white, a land owner of comfortable means, an educated man, a secure person who has a healthy self-esteem. Kumalo is black, poor, relatively uneducated, insecure except in his tribal setting where he is a respected minister.)*

2. *What circumstances bring them together? (Kumalo's son, while committing a robbery with two others, accidentally kills Jarvis' son. The two fathers meet when Kumalo seeks information from the Smiths about Sibeko's daughter, and Jarvis answers the door. Finally they come together because Jarvis owns land above the village where Kumalo is the minister. During the drought he is able to meet some of the needs of the people in the village through Kumalo's guidance.)*

3. *How are their lives parallel? (Each is a sensitive person concerned beyond his own needs and wants, loses a son, and suffers the grief caused by that loss. Each is instrumental in bringing black and white together, for Jarvis meets some of the needs of the people of Ndotsheni. The black people in turn cooperate in preparing a wreath for Jarvis when his wife dies, bringing unity among themselves in service to someone of another race.)*

4. *How are Arthur Jarvis and Absalom Kumalo contrasted? In what one way do their lives become parallel?*

(Arthur is an altruistic, wealthy white man, who desires to better the living and working conditions and the social status of black people. Absalom is a selfish, poor black youth, who is too impatient to wait for change. He is easily influenced to take reckless chances to better his situation. Each dies at the hands of the other, Jarvis by murder, Absalom by execution for that murder.)

5. Look up the Bible story of Absalom, King David's son, in II Samuel 13–19. Why do you think Alan Paton named Kumalo's son Absalom? (Each rebelled against his father to his own destruction. Each murdered someone and died by hanging, the biblical one a rather unique execution. Both fathers mourned their sons with the words "My son, Absalom," incapable of rescuing them from their fate.)

6. Absalom is also called a "prodigal". Look up that parable told by Jesus and recorded in Luke 15:11-32. Why is this an apt term applied to him? (He is wasteful of his heritage and loving childhood. He chooses the wrong companions, who cause his downfall. Finally he is sought lovingly by his father, but this father, unlike the biblical one, cannot restore him to the family circle; for the law has superseded grace.)

7. Instead of the protagonist-antagonist relationship, what framework has Paton used in developing his characters? (He has created parallel major characters, one black and one white, and parallel minor characters of the same racial contrast. The minor characters are defeated by the social situation, but the major ones gain a small victory in understanding and unity. These people are not battling one another; instead the two fathers can battle the real foe, an untenable social system, by uniting in love and concern for one another.)

8. Why is such a framework excellent for developing Paton's theme? (The real antagonist is the social system that all four characters fight. Perhaps Arthur and Absalom are too impatient to remedy something that can be changed slowly, only by degrees. As a result, they become victims of the evils in the system. The fathers learn one means to unify and cope, even if it is in an isolated village, not in a city, where it would appear that the system is the most evil. Perhaps Johannesburg is not the right place to start, for fear is too much ingrained and the scope of its evils is too broad.)

Suggested response for **Handout 12**

Taking into consideration the weaknesses of John Kumalo and his sister Gertrude, as well as their goals in life, imagine their meeting on the street after Stephen, their brother, has returned to Ndotsheni. John has thought that Gertrude returned with Stephen and her son. Write a three-page script of their conversation and then role play the scene. (Scripts will vary.)

Name _____

Date _____

Characterization

Directions: Kumalo can perhaps be termed the protagonist, but Jarvis is certainly not the antagonist, nor can any other particular person be found in that role. Answer the following questions to explore Paton's use of characters to develop his theme. Use your own paper.

1. In what ways are James Jarvis and Stephen Kumalo different?

2. What circumstances bring them together?

3. How are their lives parallel?

4. How are Arthur Jarvis and Absalom Kumalo contrasted?

5. Look up the Bible story of Absalom, King David's son, in II Samuel 13–19. Why do you think Alan Paton named Kumalo's son Absalom?

6. Absalom is also called a "prodigal". Look up that parable told by Jesus and recorded in Luke 15:11–32. Why is this an apt term applied to him?

7. Instead of the protagonist-antagonist relationship, what framework has Paton used in developing his characters?

8. Why is such a framework excellent for developing Paton's theme?

Name _____

Date _____

Two Minor Characters Meet

Directions: Taking into consideration the weaknesses of John Kumalo and his sister Gertrude as well as their goals in life, imagine their meeting on the street after Stephen, their brother, has returned to Ndotsheni. John has thought that Gertrude returned with Stephen and her son. Write a three-page script of their conversation and then role play the scene for the class.

Lesson 8
An Initiation Story

Objective

- To analyze how a person undergoing crisis develops new insights into human experience, a process in literature called the *initiation*

Notes to the Teacher

The usual *initiation* pattern takes a naive but sensitive individual and puts him/her into a new environment and a crisis experience or a series of such experiences that change him/her into a more knowledgeable person. "Naive" is used not in the sense of ignorant but in the sense of being without experience in a particular facet of life, such as grief, loneliness, rejection, and the like. Fictional characters can, of course, go through crises without noticeable change, but the initiate is a sensitive person who thinks through the things that happen and learns from them, coming out "sadder but wiser."

Procedure

1. In a class brainstorming session, list some life experiences from which students have gained understanding (for example, being in an accident, having a loved one die, getting caught in wrongdoing, moving to a new community, undergoing surgery, living through a violent storm).

2. Explain what it means to be naive in the sense of an initiate, a person who can evaluate and learn from his/her experiences.

3. Distribute **Handout 13.** Divide the class into two groups, one to deal with Stephen Kumalo as a naive but sensitive person; the other, to pinpoint various crises through which he goes, starring the most cataclysmic experience.

4. As a class, discuss what Kumalo has learned from each crisis, what specific knowledge he has gained.

Suggested responses for **Handout 13**

Kumalo as initiate - He has never been to Johannesburg, even though he is not young and is in his small village a respected leader. He has not met with many untrustworthy people and has never spent much money just to exist. Furthermore he has never had to humble himself before the white man in a subservient sense.

Crisis experiences - Kumalo journeys to Johannesburg; he is robbed by a man pretending to help him buy a ticket; he learns of his son's complicity with lawless youths; he meets rejection from his brother, who heads a dissident group; he learns of the degradation of his sister. *He experiences his son's trial and sentencing to death; he takes responsibility for his son's wife and unborn child. Other crises may be found as well; some may need to be grouped to keep from creating too long and unwieldy a list.)

Knowledge gained - He learns that the city is a frightening place and that it contains people who will take advantage of the uninitiated, that even a boy who has been brought up properly and lovingly can go astray, and that there is no reconciliation with his brother and no restoration for his sister. He must face the sadness of his son's death and the shame of having fathered a man capable of murder. He also learns what real fear is and how deeply it is ingrained in the black man's life in this society. Through the concern and help of the white priest and through the white attorney who takes Absalom's case "for God," he sees that even in the midst of oppression there are those who can love and care for others. Through Msimangu's renouncing the world's *goods and giving his savings to Kumalo, he learns that even a black man can think in terms of things more important than the material. In taking responsibility for his son's wife and unborn child, he must contemplate whether he might rear another young person dissatisfied with staying in the country or be able to prevent his grandchild from following in the footsteps of his/her father and aunt.)*

Why is the initiation story an excellent pattern for Cry, the Beloved Country? (The country person in South Africa faces some of the disadvantages of being black, mainly in that he sees the prosperity of a few white people, he hears of oppression, he has learned that his is a servile position, and he knows that he is poor. He does not, however, feel as ground under the heel of the white man as does his brother in the industrialized cities; therefore, he goes to the city hopefully and must gradually learn the true desperation of many of its people. It is doubtful that the great unity of white and black could have been shown as well as it comes out in Ndotsheni at the end of this story, and only through kindness shown him by several white people could Kumalo see hope for an ultimate national unity.)

Name _____

Date _____

Kumalo's Initiation

Directions: After a discussion of the initiation-story form. Fill in the chart below to analyze Kumalo's experience.

Kumalo as initiate - In what ways is he a naive but sensitive man?

Crisis experiences - List as many crises as you can think of.

Knowledge gained - Be specific about the things he has learned about the city, himself, others, and man in general.

Why is the initiation story an excellent pattern for *Cry, the Beloved Country?*

Lesson 9
The Importance of the Title

Objectives

- To find references to the title in the text
- To determine the ancipital, or double, meaning of the title

Notes to the teacher

Since Paton uses the words of his title several times in the text itself, it is important that students become aware of this use and seek to determine the meaning the author conveys in the title he has chosen. Eye Gate has an excellent set of filmstrips called *What to Look for in Drama and Fiction*, one of which is "Title." This filmstrip alerts the reader to the fact that the title can give important clues to the meaning of a book; it also defines the ancipital, or double, meaning of titles and gives examples. The school librarian can order it; however, most libraries already have it.

Procedure

1. View the filmstrip mentioned above if at all possible. Then discuss titles students can recall as having important clues to meaning. Discuss the ancipital edge to a title and alert them to the fact that Alan Paton has a two-edged meaning in *Cry, the Beloved Country*.

2. Distribute **Handout 14.** Ask students to answer the questions. These should lead them to an appreciation of Paton's careful choice of title. This work might best be done in small groups, or it might be done individually with findings discussed as a class for full appreciation and understanding.

   Suggested responses to **Handout** 14
   1. *Read carefully the paragraph that begins on the bottom of p.73 and concludes on the top of p.74. List five things that the narrator tells the reader are worthy of mankind's cries. How would you categorize these conditions? Why are they not eradicated? (The broken tribal society, the law and the custom that are gone, the individual man who has been murdered, the family that has been bereaved, and the fact that this is not the end of such sorrows, for man knows only fear. He sees that there are private griefs and societal griefs and makes no distinction as to importance. They are both worthy of concern and sympathy. They are worthy also of action, but apparently people just live in fear; they do not know how to act to eradicate these sufferings.)*
   2. *Read the starred passages beginning on p.78, "and some cry," and ending on p.79, "we shall not think about it at all." How is cry used in this passage? What are some of the solutions posed here? What is the greatest dilemma the white man faces? (Cry is used to mean shout or proclaim either by word or action. Some of these cries are for a completely segregated land, for more education, the restoration of the tribal life, a moral transformation. The big dilemma is that while the white man declares his superiority, he lives in fear both for his life and for what will happen if the social structure of his country changes, for the whites are greatly outnumbered by blacks.)*
   3. *On p.80 is another starred passage, beginning with "Cry, the beloved country." For whom does the narrator fear? Why? (He fears for coming generations, for they will love this beautiful land too, and such a love is dangerous in an ugly and evil political climate.)*
   4. *Paton also uses the phrase beloved country in a deliberate manner on p.222. What uniquely African custom does he cite in this passage?*

What is the beauty of this custom? Why would one cry about it? (The custom is the Zulu chant that lets neighbors know of an important happening; those people send the message on until everyone in the village or valley gets the news. In this case it is a comfort to Kumalo, for it tells that he is safely returned from Johannesburg and that the people are glad he is back. Such an interest in one's neighbors and support for a local leader is hard to find in the modern world.)

5. In still another starred passage, found on p.225 and beginning with "Yes, God save Africa," Paton also uses the phrase beloved country. If God is to save Africa, what does the narrator say must happen? (African white people must repent of their oppression of blacks and have those sins cleansed. Blacks must be saved from their lawless behavior that retaliates against whites. All must be saved from their fear, which keeps them from practicing true justice and causes them to continue in opposition to one another.)

6. After looking at these passages, write a paragraph that explains your understanding of the importance of Alan Paton's choice of the title Cry, the Beloved Country. Be sure to include your recognition of his ancipital meaning. (Answers will vary.)

Title: An Ancipital Edge

Directions: In the space provided, answer the questions:

1. Read carefully the paragraph that begins on the bottom of p.73 and concludes on the top of p.74. List five things that the narrator tells the reader are worthy of man's cries. How would you categorize these conditions? Why are they not eradicated?

2. Read the starred passages beginning on p.78, "and some cry," and ending on p.79, "we shall not think about it at all." How is *cry* used in this passage? What are some of the solutions posed here? What is the greatest dilemma the white man faces?

3. On p.80 is another starred passage, beginning with "Cry, the beloved country." For whom does the narrator fear? Why?

4. Paton also uses the phrase *beloved country* in a deliberate manner on p.222. What uniquely African custom does he cite in this passage? What is the beauty of this custom? Why would one cry about it?

5. In still another starred passage, found on p.225 and beginning with "Yes, God save Africa," Paton also uses the phrase *beloved country*. If God is to save Africa, what does the narrator say must happen?

6. After looking at these passages, write a paragraph that explains your understanding of the importance of Alan Paton's choice of the title *Cry, the Beloved Country.* Be sure to include your recognition of his ancipital meaning.

Lesson 10

Metaphor and Irony

Objectives

- To find examples of two literary devices used by the author
- To detect how they add to the reader's understanding

Notes to the Teacher

Alan Paton has used many literary devices, but for this analysis only two will be considered: *metaphor* and *irony*. A good short lesson could be done on *foreshadowing* and *prophecy*; in fact, a filmstrip on that topic, part of the set mentioned in Lesson 9, uses as one of its examples Kumalo's wife's prophecy about people who go to Johannesburg. The choice to highlight *metaphor* and *irony* is first one of exercising options and second of recognizing those devices that have sustained use in the novel. Some students may well need a review of the other devices as well.

Procedure

1. Define *metaphor*. (A figure of speech that implies an analogy. A *simple metaphor* may occur just once to create a picture for the reader; a *sustained*, or *controlling*, metaphor functions throughout an entire work. The latter is the one considered here.)

2. Distribute **Handout 15.** Instruct students to consider various quotations referring to Johannesburg. Individually they should be able to determine what the author implies by what he states directly about the city. Finally, they should draw conclusions about Paton's use of Johannesburg as a *sustained*, or *controlling*, metaphor.

3. Distribute **Handout 16.** Define *irony*. Students should probably take notes, since to complete the handout they will have to be working with various devices by which irony is achieved. (*Irony* is a figure of speech which states something that has the opposite intent. Irony of event occurs when the outcomes are the opposite of

what one expects to happen. Some common examples of irony of statement are praise that implies blame, blame that implies praise, grim humor, understatement, sarcasm, and hyperbole, which sometimes becomes caricature.)

In working on this handout, it might be well to divide the class into three groups, each having five quotations to examine. The discussion that follows, when they share their understandings, may give new insight to those who do not really find the implied meaning.)

Suggested responses for **Handout 15**

1. Consider the following quotations about Johannesburg. It might be wise to look them up, even those quoted in their entirety, since context is important to the meaning. What is implied by each?
    a. *Kumalo's wife (p.8) - "When people go to Johannesburg, they do not come back." (She has lost loved ones to a city that changes their lives and causes them to despise their roots.)*
    b. *Narrator (p.10) - "All roads lead to Johannesburg." (It is the main industrial city, the center of South African life.)*
    c. *Narrator (p.12) - "They say it is dangerous to cross the street, yet one must needs cross it. . . . The wife of Mpanza. . .saw her son Michael killed in the street." (The country people find even crossing the street a dangerous experience. This may also foreshadow Absalom's death, for unwary people are killed in Johannesburg.)*
    d. *Narrator (p.14) - "People looked at him with interest and respect, at the man who went so often to Johannesburg." (There is prestige in knowing the big city; also there is deception, for Kumalo has never been to the city before,*

49

but he enjoys the respect accorded to one who has been there often. It perhaps foreshadows the bigger deception that occurs when Kumalo leads his brother John to think that John is being betrayed by a friend.)

e. Msimangu (pp. 23-24) - "But there should be another kind of quiet in a man, . . . But in Johannesburg it is hard sometimes to find that kind of quiet." (It is a place where people seldom find calm and peace of mind.)

f. Narrator (p.32) - "One day in Johannesburg, and already the tribe was being rebuilt, the house and the soul restored." (It would seem that Kumalo is successful, for he has already found Gertrude and brought her to shelter. As the reader knows, that is a deceptive security, not a good omen; for she does not accompany him to Ndotsheni, and he will not be able to rescue Absalom. The tribe is not really being restored.)

g. John Kumalo (p.36) - "It is breaking apart, your tribal society. It is here in Johannesburg that the new society is being built." (One hopes that the new society is not so riddled with fear and violence as that seen in Johannesburg, but one fears that what appears to be praise really points out the underlying problem.)

h. Narrator (p.52, paragraph 1) - "All roads. . .delivered in Johannesburg." (People think that Johannesburg will solve all their problems, those that can be mentioned openly and those that should be kept secret. A person can find safety in anonymity. The truth is that such anonymity keeps Kumalo from finding Absalom in time.)

i. Narrator (pp.57-58) "- Shanty Town . . . have mercy upon us." (The description reveals the actual situation the black man encounters when he moves to Johannesburg.)

j. Narrator (p.65) - "The black people were not allowed to have petrol stations in Orlando." (The races are segretated.)

k. Stephen Kumalo (p. 107) - "They said, this is Johannesburg, this is a boy going wrong, as other boys have gone wrong in Johannesburg. But to us, for whom it was life and death, it was not revealed." (The large city has possibilities for both good and evil, and the uninitiated is the most vulnerable. Again the anonymity of the big city works against the country man.)

l. Narrator (p. 172) - "No second Johannesburg is needed upon the earth. One is enough." (There is so much evil, confusion, and violence that no one would wish this situation on anyone.)

m. Newspaper headline (p. 192) - "ANOTHER MURDER TRAGEDY IN CITY. EUROPEAN HOUSEHOLDER SHOT DEAD BY NATIVE HOUSEBREAKER." (The white man fears the black man, because some have become lawless. Also, as the stout woman comments immediately after this headline, it is a bad omen so close to Absalom's sentencing.)

n. Narrator (p. 230) - "Kumalo came to himself with a start and realized how far he had traveled since that journey to Johannesburg." (Kumalo has journeyed in more ways than travel; he has been initiated into the depths of man's capability for being inhumane to his fellowmen.)

o. Narrator, speaking of Kumalo (p. 241) - "He opened Msimangu's letter, and read about all the happenings of Johannesburg and was astonished to find within himself a faint nostalgia for that great bewildering city." (Even though it harbors much evil, Kumalo met with real kindness both from black and white in the city; therefore he longs for the good experiences. Also the words convey the fascination that a large, busy city has for a person who has known nothing but a simple, country life.)

  p. Narrator (p.216) - "But Gertrude was gone." (This is a well-written understatement with heartache buried deep inside.)

2. After studying the surface and implied meanings of each of the quotations, write a paragraph that explains Paton's metaphorical use of Johannesburg. (Answers will vary, but basically it is a magnetic force that draws many people and keeps them in motion. It drives some to evil and destruction and others to a new knowledge about themselves. People who go there are never the same; many never return. Finally it is a city of privation and fear: the black man is forbidden to own business or residential property in certain parts and quickly becomes the white man's dog or work animal; the white man lives in fear of retaliation. No one is safe; few are at peace.)

3. (An optional enrichment activity) Metaphor can take the form of personification, as it does in Paton's descriptions of the land. Find examples that show his seeing the land as if it were a person. (Two examples are its red hills standing desolate, the earth "torn away like flesh," the dead streams coming to life, not to sustain but to run with the "red blood of the earth.")

Suggested Responses for **Handout** 16
After the class discussion about *irony* as applied to literature, comment in writing about the irony found in each of the following:
A. Irony of event
  1. Why is it ironic that Arthur Jarvis is the one who is murdered? (He has spent his adulthood trying to better the lot of black people. He should have been venerated by them, not killed by a black youth.

On p.140 his father says, "Here he was, day in and day out, on a kind of mission. And it was he who was killed.")

  2. Why is the verdict in Absalom's trial ironic? (He had not intended to kill Arthur, but there was no provision for a black man whose act was not premeditated. Because he told the truth, he had to die. Johannes Pafuri and Matthew Kumalo, who lied, went free because no one could really prove they had been there, even though the black servant identified Pafuri. The latter two planned the robbery, but they were lucky enough not to have killed a white man.)

  3. Why is the ending of the story pleasingly ironic? (One would think that the father of the murdered man would shun the father of the murderer, but this compassionate pair show that love can overcome fear and hate. These are men who realize that the enemy is bigger than one individual and must be conquered at every level.)

  4. A more subtle situation is found in the narrator's comment about what John Kumalo says (p. 186). He says, "Something is coming," and the narrator comments that he "speaks the one meaning, and means the other meaning." What are the two meanings? How does such a statement create an irony of situation? (He speaks as if something great is coming to liberate the black people, but really all he wants is greatness for himself, the power to be acclaimed a leader.)

  5. Why is it ironic that Arthur Jarvis apparently studied and revered Abraham Lincoln? (Both died trying to give the black people their rights, and both were murdered needlessly.)
B. Irony of statement

1. Read Chapter 23, where the author's tongue-in-cheek description and comments are full of ironies that seem to praise while they blame. Find at least five and show why they are ironic. (Ones given below are merely representative.)

   a. (On p.167, the discovery of gold gets more attention than the murder trial, implying that man overrates the value of wealth.)

   b. (On p.168, the unpronounceable names are only such because the person commenting is English, not an Afrikaner.)

   c. (On p.170, the men who make the money in the mines do not do the back-breaking work, but they are commended for their courage, foresight, and mental strain while cheating others.)

   d. (Also on p.170, the men with big art collections who go to their ranches to hunt and thus "feel one with Nature" really know nothing about the deteriorating condition of the land, how they are ruining the balance of nature with their wasteful sport, and how their use of wealth really deprives people of a decent way of life.)

   e. (On p.171, over-vitaminizing the natives is ridiculous. No one is providing for them at all, neither decent housing nor food is given them.)

2. (P.187) "Perhaps we should thank God he [John Kumalo] is corrupt, said Msimangu solemnly. For if he were not corrupt, he could plunge this country into bloodshed." What does he mean? Why is this statement ironic? (He means that Kumalo will stop just short of putting his own life in danger. All he really wants is the power to sway people. If he were really an honest crusader, he would put his life on the line and therefore lead others to death for a cause. Msimangu apparently believes it is too early for the blacks to gain anything, for they have not found the right leader. The result of a disorganized uprising would be mass death.)

3. (P.149) Comment on the irony in this statement made by the older Harrison: "We're not safe, Jarvis. I don't even know that stringing 'em up will make us safe. Sometimes I think it's got beyond us." (He seriously advocates Ku Klux Klan methods, yet ironically he is right; such tactics won't help. The situation is beyond the white man, yes; but it has been that way a long time and will get worse. As a typical white Englishman in isolation from the real world, he just hasn't realized the deterioration that has been developing.)

4. What is ironic about Harrison's saying (p. 150), "But the natives as a whole are getting out of hand. They've even started Trade Unions, did you know that?" (He actually acknowledges the double standard set up for the races; white laborers have a voice in their working conditions; black laborers are treated like work animals. This again is a beautifully phrased understatement.)

5. Read paragraph 2 on p.151. How are his statements about the mines and a republic ironic? (He thinks that giving South Africa up to the natives would be the only way they could have power, yet that is the "worst-case" scenario. He never has considered some granting of human rights. If there were a republic, the blacks would have a vote, and the whites would either be out of power or have to share it.)

Literary Devices: Metaphor and Irony

Directions: Write answers:

1. Consider the following quotations about Johannesburg. It might be wise to look them up, even those quoted in their entirety, since context is important to the meaning. What is implied by each?
   a. Kumalo's wife (p.8) - "When people go to Johannesburg, they do not come back."
   b. Narrator (p.10) - "All roads lead to Johannesburg."
   c. Narrator (p.12) - "They say it is dangerous to cross the street, yet one must cross it. . . . The wife of Mpanza . . . saw her son Michael killed in the street."
   d. Narrator (p.14) - "People looked at him with interest and respect, at the man who went so often to Johannesburg."
   e. Msimangu (pp.23-24) - "But there should be another kind of quiet in a man. . . . But in Johannesburg it is hard sometimes to find that kind of quiet."
   f. Narrator (p.32) - "One day in Johannesburg, and already the tribe was being re-built, the house and the soul restored."
   g. John Kumalo (p.36) - "It is breaking apart, your tribal society. It is here in Johannesburg that the new society is being built."
   h. Narrator (p.52, paragraph 1) - "All roads . . . delivered in Johannesburg."
   i. Narrator (pp.57-58) "- Shanty Town . . . have mercy upon us."
   j. Narrator (p.65) - "The black people were not allowed to have petrol stations in Orlando."
   k. Stephen Kumalo (p.107) - "They said, this is Johannesburg, this is a boy going wrong, as other boys have gone wrong in Johannesburg. But to us, for whom it was life and death, it was not revealed."
   l. Narrator (p.172) - "No second Johannesburg is needed upon the earth. One is enough."
   m. Newspaper headline (p.192) - "ANOTHER MURDER TRAGEDY IN THE CITY. EUROPEAN HOUSEHOLDER SHOT DEAD BY NATIVE HOUSEBREAKER."
   n. Narrator (p.230) - "Kumalo came to himself with a start and realized how far he had traveled since that journey to Johannesburg."
   o. Narrator, speaking of Kumalo (p.241) - "He opened Msimangu's letter, and read about all the happenings of Johannesburg and was astonished to find within himself a faint nostalgia for that great bewildering city."
   p. Narrator (p.216) - "But Gertrude was gone."

2. After studying the surface and implied meanings of each of the quotations, write a paragraph that explains Paton's metaphorical use of Johannesburg.

3. (An optional enrichment activity) Metaphor can take the form of personification, as it does in Paton's descriptions of the land. Find examples that show his seeing this land as if it were a person.

Name _____

Date _____

Ironic Happenings and Statements

Directions: Answer the following questions. Use your own paper.

A. Irony of Event

1. Why is it ironic that Arthur Jarvis is the one who is murdered?
2. Why is the verdict in Absalom's trial ironic?
3. Why is the ending of the story pleasantly ironic?
4. A more subtle situation is found in the narrator's comment about what John Kumalo says (p.186). He says, "Something is coming," and the narrator comments that he "speaks the one meaning, and means the other meaning." What are the two meanings? How does such a statement create an irony of situation?
5. Why is it ironic that Arthur Jarvis apparently studied and revered Abraham Lincoln?

B. Irony of Statement

1. Read Chapter 23, where the author's tongue-in-cheek description and comments are full of ironies that seem to praise while they blame. Find at least five and show why they are ironic.

    a.

    b.

    c.

    d.

    e.

2. (P.187) "Perhaps we should thank God he [John Kumalo] is corrupt, said Msimangu solemnly. For if he were not corrupt, he could plunge this country into bloodshed." What does he mean? Why is this statement ironic?
3. (P.149) Comment on the irony in this statement made by the older Harrison: "We're not safe, Jarvis. I don't even know that stringing 'em up will make us safe. Sometimes I think it's got beyond us."
4. What is ironic about Harrison's saying (p.150), "But the natives as a whole are getting out of hand. They've even started Trade Unions, did you know that?"
5. Read paragraph 2 on p.151. How are his statements about the mines and a republic ironic?

Lesson 11
The Beloved Country Still Causes Tears

Objective

- To compare the South African situation as depicted in 1948 by Alan Paton to the present situation

Notes to the Teacher

Lesson 1 dealt briefly with the historical background of South Africa to give the students some understanding of the political and social setting for the novel. Some updating of the situation will show how timely Alan Paton's writing is today. The problem with this lesson is that the questions may be easily outdated by things that are happening even as the novel is being studied. It is important, however, to recognize the prophetic insight of a perceptive author.

Procedure

1. If possible, get a copy of "Rocking the Cradle of the Volk," in TIME (May 4, 1987) and of "Children on the Front Line," in NEWSWEEK (July 27, 1987). In addition students should read the latest magazine and newspaper articles on South Africa, using the *Readers' Guide* as one source of such listings.

2. Distribute **Handout 17.** Use it as a partial guide, adding other items as necessary to update the material. Note that question 6 can be used as a springboard for a class discussion or for a debate, the latter being an activity that differs somewhat from the many discussions in this unit.

   Suggested Responses for **Handout** 17
   1. *Read the last five paragraphs of Arthur Jarvis' manuscript, found toward the end of Chapter 20 (p.146). How true is this description today? (Answers will vary according to the amount of progress made.)*
   2. *Harrison says in Chapter 21 (p.150), "But the natives as a whole are get-*

ting out of hand." He spoke of labor unions. What similar new developments could cause a white South African to make the same comment today? (Answers will vary.)
   3. *Read the passage that ends Jarvis' manuscript in Chapter 21 (pp.154-155). Which parts of this passage have seen some progress in South Africa? in the United States? Which statements still hold true even today? (Answers will vary.)*
   4. *At the end of Chapter 7 (first full paragraph on p. 40), Msimangu says, "I have one great fear in my heart, that one day when they are turned to loving, they will find that we are turned to hating."*

The Kansas City Star *for November 9, 1986 (p.1K), contained an interesting article about Alan Paton and his feelings about the accuracy with which he had predicted the events that we see in South Africa today. The closing paragraph of that article contains the following observation:*

"There is the psychological difficulty of the conqueror living on equal terms with the conquered. I'm not sure Americans can understand how difficult that is going to be. The line I wrote about the blacks having turned to hating—I am sorry to say that those were prophetic words."

What specific events would cause the author to make these comments? (Answers will vary, but included should be the 1976 Soweto uprising and the 1986 fighting with knives, pipes, and rocks thrown by young black radicals outside Cape Town's Crossroads shantytown, the goldminer's strike in August 1987, that crippled the economy of South Africa, and other similar uprisings. If Kaffir Boy—see #7 below—is available, note particularly what Chapters 41 and 43 have to say about modern black youths in South Africa.)

5. In what ways have black South Africans gained a better way of life? If you feel that there is no improvement, be specific about conditions that have not changed. (Answers will vary. One worthy of note is the Lebowa Bakery Company, the first black-owned business to be entered into the South African stock market, a company grossing in the millions and even having white men working under black bosses.)

6. One continuing problem is the role other countries play in this situation. Some companies have withdrawn their industries and holdings from South Africa. Others say that they will stay because leaving ends their influence: they no longer have a voice in making change. Paton himself said in the Star article, mentioned in question 4, that economic sanctions such as the United States Congress approved in 1987 merely compound the misery. Many say all these actions simply mean fewer jobs for black workers. List arguments for both positions. Which do you consider valid? Why? (Answers will vary. This might be a good topic for class discussion or for a lively debate between astute class members. Note particularly Shell Oil's decision not to move out in 1987.)

7. (An optional enrichment activity) Read Kaffir Boy, an autobiography by Mark Mathabane (New York: Macmillan Publishing Company, 1986). It is an account about growing up black in South Africa that has been likened to Richard Wright's Native Son. Since it is a biography, it might more accurately be compared to Wright's Black Boy. Consult your teacher about the best way to report your findings to the class. If you or your friends have read Native Son or Black Boy, it might be interesting to compare the American and the South African experience.

The Beloved Country Still Causes Tears

Directions. Before beginning work on this handout, it would be wise to read "Rocking the Cradle of the Volk," in TIME (May 4, 1987) and "Children on the Front Line," NEWSWEEK (July 27, 1987), as well as other recent articles listed in the *READERS' GUIDE.*

Answer the questions. Use your own paper.

1. Read the last five paragraphs of Arthur Jarvis' manuscript, found toward the end of Chapter 20 (p.146). How true is this description today?

2. Harrison says in Chapter 21 (p.150), "But the natives as a whole are getting out of hand." He spoke of labor unions. What similar new developments could cause a white South African to make the same comment today?

3. Read the passage that ends Jarvis' manuscript in Chapter 21 (pp.154-155). Which parts of this passage have seen some progress in South Africa? in the United States? Which statements still hold true even today?

4. At the end of Chapter 7 (first full paragraph on p.40), Msimangu says, "I have one great fear in my heart, that one day when they are turned to loving, they will find that we are turned to hating."

   The *Kansas City Star* for November 9, 1986, (p.1K), contained an interesting article about Alan Paton and his feelings about the accuracy with which he had predicted the events we see in South Africa today. The closing paragraph of that article contains the following observation:

   > "There is the psychological difficulty of the conqueror living on equal terms with the conquered. I'm not sure Americans can understand how difficult that is going to be. The line I wrote about the blacks having turned to hating—I am sorry to say that those were prophetic words."

   What specific events would cause the author to make these comments?

5. In what ways have black South Africans gained a better way of life? If you feel that there is no improvement, be specific about conditions that have not changed.

6. One continuing problem is the role other countries play in this situation. Some companies have withdrawn their industries and holdings from South Africa. Others say that they will stay because leaving ends their influence; they no longer have a voice in making changes. Paton himself said in the *Star* article, mentioned in question 4, that economic sanctions such as the United States Congress approved in 1987 merely compound the misery. Many say all these actions simply mean fewer jobs for black workers. List arguments for both positions. Which do you consider valid? Why?

7. (An optional enrichment activity) Read *Kaffir Boy*, an autobiography by Mark Mathabane (New York: Macmillan Publishing Company, 1986). It is an account about growing up black in South Africa that has been likened to Richard Wright's *Native Son*, which is a biography, and might more accurately be compared to Wright's *Black Boy*. Consult your teacher about the best way to report your findings to the class. If you or your friends have read *Native Son* or *Black Boy*, it might be interesting to compare the American and South African experiences.

Lesson 12
Values That Govern Actions and Relationships

Objective

- To detect how without heavy-handed moralizing, Paton has revealed the values that govern the lives of his characters

Notes to the Teacher

It is impossible to ferret out all the values that form the foundation of *Cry, the Beloved Country*, but students can benefit from taking note of how the value systems various characters live by govern their actions, attitudes, and relationships.

The following pages contain statements that reveal life values:

108	212	257, 258
167	213	262
168 & 171	227	265
169	229	266
174	233	267
175	245	269
182	247	272
186	248	274

Procedure

1. Divide the class into groups of three or four students each. At first let them brainstorm about values they observed through reading and studying the novel.

2. Put the pages listed above on the chalkboard, on newsprint, or on an overhead transparency so that they are clearly visible.

3. Distribute **Handout 18.** It might be wise to give a certain number of pages to each group so that all students do not need to go over the whole book in a very time-consuming search. Once the groups have filled in those values that were discovered in the brainstorming session, they should look for the specific things they find in a careful reading of the pages assigned to them. These should be added to the chart provided in the handout.

4. When all groups are finished, they should each report their findings for others to complete their charts. It might be good to make an overhead transparency of the chart so that a master listing exists for those who may not grasp details as they are reported.

Suggested Responses for **Handout 18** (The numbers in parentheses indicate pages.)

1. *Charting Values*

   CONSTRUCTIVE:
   Home and land, Kumalo and Jarvis
   Absence of fear, Kumalo, Msimangu, and both Jarvises
   Life and family, Absalom, after it is too late
   Sorrow that enriches (108), Father Vincent
   Interracial understanding (174) and life goal (175), Arthur Jarvis
   Helping the poor and preserving son's memory (213), Jarvis Prayer (229), Kumalo
   Restoration of land, especially Ndotsheni (233), Kumalo
   Preservation of language and culture (248), Kumalo and Arthur's son
   Love (258), Kumalo and Jarvis
   Understanding (272–74), Jarvis and Kumalo
   Improved living and working conditions, black people
   Honor, charity and generosity (174), the Jarvis family
   Kindness (182), James Jarvis
   Cleansing, purifying and God's mercy (212), Stephen Kumalo
   Ability to bear suffering (227), Kumalo's native friend
   Compassion (245, 262 and 269), Jarvis
   Education (247, 265), black people
   Sympathy (257–258), Kumalo and the black church congregation

Hope (266), people of the valley
Awareness of God and His goodness
(274), Kumalo

(These attributes can be held by more people than the ones specifically mentioned here; those listed are the ones that expressed these values on the pages given).

DESTRUCTIVE

White man's possessions, black men, especially the city youth
Cattle as wealth, native farmers
Gold (167), white race
Profit (169), white race
Power (186), John Kumalo
Freedom that means license, Absalom and friends

Supremacy, all races and nationalities
Supremacy with segregation from Afrikaners
and blacks (168 and 171), English
Pride (267), young agricultural demonstrator
(Of course, other possibilities exist)

2. Write a paragraph in which you choose the most destructive value you found and explain why you chose it. It may encompass other negatives, values that become spinoffs of the primary one.

3. Write a second paragraph about the most important value you would like to develop and explain why you chose it.

Name _____

Date _____

Values That Govern Actions and Relationships

Directions: It is impossible to ferret out all the values, both constructive and destructive, that form the foundation of *Cry, the Beloved Country.* It is, however, beneficial to analyze the values that govern the actions and relationships of some of Paton's characters. You are asked to study the pages assigned to you to find statements that imply or directly state certain people's values. Write these in the appropriate columns. You will not have completed your chart until all groups have reported their findings.

1. Charting values

CONSTRUCTIVE		DESTRUCTIVE	
The value itself	The person(s)	The value itself	The person(s)

2. Write a paragraph in which you choose the most destructive value you found and explain why you chose it. It may encompass other negatives, values that become spin-offs.

3. Write a second paragraph about the most important value you would like to develop and explain why you chose it.

Name _____

Date _____

Unit Test I

A. Matching - Put the letter of the correct description in the blank before each name or word.

_____ 1. Stephen Kumalo

a. The lawyer who took the case of the parson's son "pro deo" (for God)

_____ 2. Absalom Kumalo

b. a title used in respect, "parson"

_____ 3. James Jarvis

c. Stephen Kumalo's sister

_____ 4. Arthur Jarvis

d. a title meaning "sir"

_____ 5. Msimangu

e. a wealthy white land owner

_____ 6. Mrs. Lithebe

f. open grass country

_____ 7. Umfundisi

g. Xosa word for the Great Spirit

_____ 8. Ndotsheni

h. the servant of the murdered man

_____ 9. Tixo

i. a loving woman who rented a room to the parson

_____ 10. Umnumzana

j. the man who was murdered

_____ 11. Velt

k. a country parson

_____ 12. Gertrude

l. the rosy-cheeked English priest

_____ 13. Mr. Mafolo

m. the minister who helped the parson find his son

_____ 14. Mr. Carmichael

n. the parson's son

_____ 15. Father Vincent

o. the man who led the parson to the Mission House

p. the village from which the parson came

Name _____

Date _____

B. Short Answer - Answer concisely but completely each of the following questions:

    1. Msimangu says that the government is more afraid of Dubula then it is of Tomlinson or John Kumalo. Why is this statement true?

    2. Why does Gertrude never reach the parson's country home?

    3. *Fear* is a recurring word in the novel. By using specific examples, explain what you consider to be the greatest fear of the black people, the white people.

    4. Describe briefly the solution to this fear by citing *three* specific examples that Paton uses, people and their actions that successfully combat fear and hatred.

Unit Test II (Final Exam)

I. Choose one of the following quotations as a topic for a paragraph of about a hundred words, explaining what it means and its significance to the action of the novel. (Use your own paper.)

A. James Jarvis says, "I have seen a man who was in darkness . . . till you found him."

B. Msimangu says, "When a man loves, he seeks no power, and therefore he has power."

C. Father Vincent says, "Fear is a journey, a terrible journey, but sorrow is at least an arriving."

II. It is easy to consider this novel as dealing merely with the South African dilemma, yet Paton, by using Arthur Jarvis' interest in Abraham Lincoln, gives it a broader interpretation by linking it to our own country's problem with slavery. Also he gives many clues to indicate that he is thinking beyond just the racial issue in any one place or time.

Write an essay of about 200 words that discusses the universality of the novel's theme and characters. In your essay do not deal with the social or racial problems as such; instead decide what the novel says about human experience and the motivation for human actions. Then use specific examples from your own experience or knowledge of human behavior to show that Paton's characters and theme have universality, that they are representative of people in other situations.

Answers to Unit Tests I and II

Unit Test I

A. Matching

1. k	6. i	11. f
2. n	7. b	12. c
3. e	8. p	13. o
4. j	9. g	14. a
5. m	10. d	15. l

B. Short Answer

1. Msimangu says that the government is more afraid of Dubula than it is of Tomlinson or John Kumalo. Why is this statement true? (John Kumalo wants the power and loves to hear himself talk, but behind the bluster is an easily frightened man whose main interest is protecting himself. Tomlinson has brains, but Dubula has heart. The latter has a deep conviction about what is right, and he is not afraid or self-seeking; therefore he is capable of leading people even to their deaths for a cause. Such people can bring change through open revolution.)

2. Why does Gertrude never reach the parson's country home? (She cannot leave the city and its attractions, even if she must continue a life of prostitution.)

3. *Fear* is a recurring word in the novel. By using specific examples, explain what you consider to be the greatest fear of the black people, the white people. (Answers will vary, and any that are carefully backed by examples from the text are acceptable. Perhaps for blacks it is apartheid itself, for it causes inequalities such as slum housing, work passes, worthless land, and injustice in the courts. The whites fear losing their position of superiority and thus fear violence, threats to their lives, giving up any power or privilege, and changing laws to give equal justice to black people.)

4. Describe briefly the solution to this fear by citing *three* specific examples that Paton uses, people and their actions that successfully combat fear and hatred. (Answers will vary. One might cite Msimangu, who helps Kumalo find his son and then gives his money to Kumalo when he himself adopts a life of meditation. Another is James Jarvis, who learns to love the black people after reading his son's manuscript and helps the people of Ndotsheni by having a dam built to provide water and by promising to build them a church. A third might be Stephen Kumalo, who never blames the white man even though the system has corrupted his son, his brother, and his sister and has robbed his people of the right to have a decent life.)

Unit Test II (Final Exam)

1. Choose one of the following quotations as a topic for a paragraph of about a hundred words, explaining what it means and its significance to the action of the novel.
   A. James Jarvis says, "I have seen a man who was in darkness . . . till you found him." (This quotation, found on p.272, voices well the sensitive white person's dilemma. Jarvis is the man who was in darkness, for he had never before really come in contact with the black man's situation. Once he reads his son's viewpoint and meets

the humble and sincere Kumalo, he wants to help the black people, for he sees their victimization. He conquers hate and fear through love and understanding. The significance is that there has been no real communication between the races; apartheid is possible because black people seldom see the luxurious life of the whites, who in turn never think about the oppression of the blacks. Fear of each other and blindness to the other's viewpoint cause violence, destruction, and death.)

B. Msimangu says, "When a man loves, he seeks no power, and therefore he has power." (This quotation, on p.39, states the sore need of South Africa, a man who loves and understands both white and black and therefore can bridge the gap between them. Violence will engender greater hatred and destruction; people like John Kumalo, who need power to bolster their own egos, will prove to be cowards when confronted by those more powerful than they. Only the true humanitarian will hazard his life for a cause. He attracts those with a similar motivation and causes fear in those who have more selfish reasons to act.)

C. Father Vincent says, "Fear is a journey, a terrible journey, but sorrow is at least an arriving." (These words, spoken on p.108, show the superiority of sorrow over fear. Fear always makes one poorer, but sorrow, if properly handled, can enrich a person. People who know devastating sorrow, as Stephen Kumalo and James Jarvis do in the loss of their sons, can take one of two directions: they can fear each other and the other race more, or they can use the tenderness that comes with a broken heart to open themselves to each other. Because they have already experienced the greatest loss, they can see the folly of putting high value on things of lesser importance. They have arrived at a new sense of values, seeing human relationships as they should be.)

II. It is easy to consider this novel as dealing merely with the South African dilemma, yet Paton, by using Arthur Jarvis' interest in Abraham Lincoln, gives it a broader interpretation by linking it to our own country's problem with slavery. Also he gives many clues to indicate that he is thinking beyond just the racial issue in any one place or time.

Write an essay of about 200 words that discusses the universality of the novel's theme and characters. In your essay do not deal with the social or racial problems as such; instead decide what the novel says about human experience and the motivation for human actions. Then use specific examples from your own experience or knowledge of human behavior to show that Paton's characters and theme have universality, that they are representative of people in other situations.

(Answers will vary, but there are many who grasp power as John Kumalo did, many who impatiently take the law in their own hands as the three black youths did, many truthful people who like Absalom find themselves caught while liars go free, a few who lead from sincere belief in a cause as Arthur Jarvis and Dubula did, and a very few who bridge the gap between the races as James Jarvis and Stephen Kumalo did; but those few find some solutions and inner peace. Specific examples will vary.)

Acknowledgments

For permission to reprint all works in this volume by each of the following authors, grateful acknowledgment is made to the holders of copyright, publishers, or representatives named below.

Lesson 5
Excerpt from *A Handbook to Literature* by Thrall and Hibbard, 1961. Published by The Odyssey Press, New York, New York.

Lesson 10 and 11
Excerpts from *Cry, the Beloved Country* by Alan Paton, 1948. Published by Macmillan Publishing Co., Inc., New York, New York.

Novel/Drama Series

Novel

*Absolutely Normal Chaos/
    Chasing Redbird*, Creech

Across Five Aprils, Hunt

Adam of the Road, Gray/*Catherine,
    Called Birdy*, Cushman

The Adventures of Huckleberry Finn,
    Twain

The Adventures of Tom Sawyer, Twain

*Alice's Adventures in Wonderland/
    Through the Looking-Glass*, Carroll

All Creatures Great and Small, Herriot

All Quiet on the Western Front,
    Remarque

All the King's Men, Warren

Animal Farm, Orwell/
    The Book of the Dun Cow,
    Wangerin, Jr.

Anna Karenina, Tolstoy

Anne Frank: The Diary of a Young Girl,
    Frank

Anne of Green Gables, Montgomery

April Morning, Fast

The Assistant/The Fixer, Malamud

*The Autobiography of Miss Jane
    Pittman*, Gaines

The Awakening, Chopin/
    Madame Bovary, Flaubert

Babbitt, Lewis

The Bean Trees/Pigs in Heaven,
    Kingsolver

Beowulf/Grendel, Gardner

Billy Budd/Moby Dick, Melville

Black Boy, Wright

Bless Me, Ultima, Anaya

Brave New World, Huxley

The Bridge of San Luis Rey, Wilder

The Brothers Karamazov, Dostoevsky

The Call of the Wild/White Fang,
    London

The Canterbury Tales, Chaucer

The Catcher in the Rye, Salinger

The Cay/Timothy of the Cay, Taylor

Charlotte's Web, White/
    The Secret Garden, Burnett

The Chosen, Potok

The Christmas Box, Evans/
    A Christmas Carol, Dickens

Chronicles of Narnia, Lewis

Cold Sassy Tree, Burns

The Count of Monte Cristo, Dumas

Crime and Punishment, Dostoevsky

Cry, the Beloved Country, Paton

Dandelion Wine, Bradbury

Darkness at Noon, Koestler

David Copperfield, Dickens

Davita's Harp, Potok

A Day No Pigs Would Die, Peck

Death Comes for the Archbishop,
    Cather

December Stillness, Hahn/
    Izzy, Willy-Nilly, Voigt

The Divine Comedy, Dante

The Dollmaker, Arnow

Don Quixote, Cervantes

Dr. Zhivago, Pasternak

Dubliners, Joyce

East of Eden, Steinbeck

Ellen Foster/A Virtuous Woman,
    Gibbons

Emma, Austen

Fahrenheit 451, Bradbury

A Farewell to Arms, Hemingway

Farewell to Manzanar, Houston &
    Houston/*Black Like Me*, Griffin

Frankenstein, Shelley

*From the Mixed-up Files of Mrs. Basil
    E. Frankweiler*, Konigsburg/*The
    Westing Game*, Raskin

A Gathering of Flowers, Thomas, ed.

The Giver, Lowry

The Good Earth, Buck

The Grapes of Wrath, Steinbeck

Great Expectations, Dickens

The Great Gatsby, Fitzgerald

Gulliver's Travels, Swift

Hard Times, Dickens

Hatchet, Paulsen/*Robinson Crusoe*,
    Defoe

Having Our Say, Delany, Delany, &
    Hearth/*A Gathering of Old Men*,
    Gaines

The Heart Is a Lonely Hunter, McCullers

Heart of Darkness, Conrad

Hiroshima, Hersey/*On the Beach*, Shute

The Hobbit, Tolkien

Homecoming/Dicey's Song, Voigt

The Hound of the Baskervilles, Doyle

*The Human Comedy/
    My Name Is Aram*, Saroyan

Incident at Hawk's Hill, Eckert/
    Where the Red Fern Grows, Rawls

Invisible Man, Ellison

Jane Eyre, Brontë

Johnny Tremain, Forbes

Journey of the Sparrows, Buss/Cubias/
    The Honorable Prison, de Jenkins

The Joy Luck Club, Tan

Jubal Sackett/The Walking Drum,
    L'Amour

Julie of the Wolves, George/*Island of
    the Blue Dolphins*, O'Dell

The Jungle, Sinclair

The Killer Angels, Shaara

Le Morte D'Arthur, Malory

The Learning Tree, Parks

Les Miserables, Hugo

*The Light in the Forest/
    A Country of Strangers*, Richter

*Little House in the Big Woods/
    Little House on the Prairie*, Wilder

Little Women, Alcott

Lord of the Flies, Golding

The Lord of the Rings, Tolkien

The Martian Chronicles, Bradbury

Missing May, Rylant/*The Summer of
    the Swans*, Byars

Mrs. Mike, Freedman/*I Heard the Owl
    Call My Name*, Craven

*Murder on the Orient Express/
    And Then There Were None*, Christie

My Antonia, Cather

The Natural, Malamud/*Shoeless Joe*,
    Kinsella

Nectar in a Sieve, Markandaya/
    The Woman Warrior, Kingston

Night, Wiesel

A Night to Remember, Lord/*Streams to
    the River, River to the Sea*, O'Dell

1984, Orwell

Number the Stars, Lowry/*Friedrich*,
    Richter

Obasan, Kogawa

The Odyssey, Homer

The Old Man and the Sea,
    Hemingway/*Ethan Frome*, Wharton

The Once and Future King, White

O Pioneers!, Cather/*The Country of
    the Pointed Firs*, Jewett

Ordinary People, Guest/
    The Tin Can Tree, Tyler

The Outsiders, Hinton/
    Durango Street, Bonham

The Pearl/Of Mice and Men, Steinbeck

The Picture of Dorian Gray, Wilde/
    Dr. Jekyll and Mr. Hyde, Stevenson

The Pigman/The Pigman's Legacy,
    Zindel

*A Portrait of the Artist as a Young
    Man*, Joyce

The Power and the Glory, Greene

A Prayer for Owen Meany, Irving

Pride and Prejudice, Austen

The Prince, Machiavelli/*Utopia*, More

The Prince and the Pauper, Twain

Profiles in Courage, Kennedy

Rebecca, du Maurier

The Red Badge of Courage, Crane

Red Sky at Morning, Bradford

The Return of the Native, Hardy

A River Runs Through It, Maclean

*Roll of Thunder, Hear My Cry/
    Let the Circle Be Unbroken*, Taylor

Saint Maybe, Tyler

Sarum, Rutherfurd

The Scarlet Letter, Hawthorne

The Scarlet Pimpernel, Orczy

A Separate Peace, Knowles

*Shabanu: Daughter of the Wind/
    Haveli*, Staples

Shane, Schaefer/*The Ox-Bow
    Incident*, Van Tilburg Clark

Siddhartha, Hesse

*The Sign of the Chrysanthemum/
    The Master Puppeteer*, Paterson

*The Signet Classic Book of Southern
    Short Stories*, Abbott and
    Koppelman, eds.

The Slave Dancer, Fox/
    I, Juan de Pareja*, De Treviño

Snow Falling on Cedars, Guterson

Song of Solomon, Morrison

The Sound and the Fury, Faulkner

Spoon River Anthology, Masters

*A Stranger Is Watching/I'll Be Seeing
    You*, Higgins Clark

The Stranger/The Plague, Camus

Summer of My German Soldier, Greene/
    Waiting for the Rain, Gordon

A Tale of Two Cities, Dickens

Talking God/A Thief of Time, Hillerman

Tess of the D'Urbervilles, Hardy

Their Eyes Were Watching God,
    Hurston

Things Fall Apart/No Longer at Ease,
    Achebe

To Kill a Mockingbird, Lee

To the Lighthouse, Woolf

Travels with Charley, Steinbeck

Treasure Island, Stevenson

A Tree Grows in Brooklyn, Smith

Tuck Everlasting, Babbitt/
    Bridge to Terabithia, Paterson

The Turn of the Screw/Daisy Miller,
    James

Uncle Tom's Cabin, Stowe

Walden, Thoreau/*A Different
    Drummer*, Kelley

Walk Two Moons, Creech

Walkabout, Marshall

Watership Down, Adams

When the Legends Die, Borland

Where the Lilies Bloom, Cleaver/
    No Promises in the Wind, Hunt

Winesburg, Ohio, Anderson

The Witch of Blackbird Pond, Speare/
    My Brother Sam Is Dead, Collier
    and Collier

A Wrinkle in Time, L'Engle/*The Lion,
    the Witch and the Wardrobe*, Lewis

Wuthering Heights, Brontë

The Yearling, Rawlings/
    The Red Pony, Steinbeck

Year of Impossible Goodbyes, Choi/*So
    Far from the Bamboo Grove*, Watkins

Zlata's Diary, Filipović/
    The Lottery Rose, Hunt

Drama

Antigone, Sophocles

Arms and the Man/Saint Joan, Shaw

The Crucible, Miller

Cyrano de Bergerac, Rostand

Death of a Salesman, Miller

A Doll's House/Hedda Gabler, Ibsen

The Glass Menagerie, Williams

The Importance of Being Earnest, Wilde

Inherit the Wind, Lawrence and Lee

Long Day's Journey into Night, O'Neill

A Man for All Seasons, Bolt

Medea, Euripides/*The Lion in Winter*,
    Goldman

The Miracle Worker, Gibson

Murder in the Cathedral, Eliot/*Galileo*,
    Brecht

The Night Thoreau Spent in Jail,
    Lawrence and Lee

Oedipus the King, Sophocles

Our Town, Wilder

*The Playboy of the Western World/
    Riders to the Sea*, Synge

Pygmalion, Shaw

A Raisin in the Sun, Hansberry

1776, Stone and Edwards

She Stoops to Conquer, Goldsmith/
    The Matchmaker, Wilder

A Streetcar Named Desire, Williams

Tartuffe, Molière

*Three Comedies of American Family
    Life: I Remember Mama*, van
    Druten/*Life with Father*, Lindsay
    and Crouse/*You Can't Take It with
    You*, Hart and Kaufman

Waiting for Godot, Beckett/
    *Rosencrantz & Guildenstern Are
    Dead*, Stoppard

Shakespeare

As You Like It

Hamlet

Henry IV, Part I

Henry V

Julius Caesar

King Lear

Macbeth

The Merchant of Venice

A Midsummer Night's Dream

Much Ado about Nothing

Othello

Richard III

Romeo and Juliet

The Taming of the Shrew

The Tempest

Twelfth Night

The Center for Learning

To Order Contact: **The Center for Learning—Shipping/Business Office**
P.O. Box 910, Villa Maria, PA 16155
800-767-9090 • 724-964-8083 • Fax 888-767-8080

The Publisher

All instructional materials identified by the TAP® (Teachers/ Authors/Publishers) trademark are developed by a national network of teachers whose collective educational experience distinguishes the publishing objective of The Center for Learning, a nonprofit educational corporation founded in 1970.

Concentrating on values-related disciplines, the Center publishes humanities and religion curriculum units for use in public and private schools and other educational settings. Approximately 500 language arts, social studies, novel/drama, life issues, and faith publications are available.

While acutely aware of the challenges and uncertain solutions to growing educational problems, the Center is committed to quality curriculum development and to the expansion of learning opportunities for all students. Publications are regularly evaluated and updated to meet the changing and diverse needs of teachers and students. Teachers may offer suggestions for development of new publications or revisions of existing titles by contacting

The Center for Learning

Administrative/Editorial Office
21590 Center Ridge Road
Rocky River, OH 44116
(440) 331-1404 • FAX (440) 331-5414
E-mail: cfl@stratos.net
Web: www.centerforlearning.org

For a free catalog containing order and price information and a descriptive listing of titles, contact

The Center for Learning

Shipping/Business Office
P.O. Box 910
Villa Maria, PA 16155
(724) 964-8083 • (800) 767-9090
FAX (888) 767-8080